Something More

Something More

Stephen W. Redding

Illustrated by
Meurcie K. Redding
&
Valerie Landon Ryan

iUniverse, Inc.
New York Lincoln Shanghai

Something More

iUniverse books may be ordered through booksellers or by contacting:

iUniverse
2021 Pine Lake Road, Suite 100
Lincoln, NE 68512
www.iuniverse.com
1-800-Authors (1-800-288-4677)

ISBN-13: 978-0-595-34665-3 (pbk)
ISBN-13: 978-0-595-79410-2 (ebk)
ISBN-10: 0-595-34665-0 (pbk)
ISBN-10: 0-595-79410-6 (ebk)

Printed in the United States of America

This book is dedicated
to all of us.

Contents

Foreword

"The words and thoughts that lie herein, by Stephen Redding, are powerful. They come from life experiences that are unique and that are filled with great wisdom and insight. I believe that what Stephen has to say, and what is in his heart and mind are enlightening and profound. He was given this insight and these experiences for a reason, maybe one that is yet to be known. But I believe that it is in Stephen's ability to share these experiences with his words, speech, writings and encounters with others, that therein lies the answer to the "Why?". I am moved reading his words, as I believe others, too, will be. We are all searching in this life for the whys and the wheres and the hows, and I believe that this place can be a lonely place for all of us. Stephen's mother, whom I never had the honor to know, was quite a woman, who was open to and connected to the spiritual, less tangible aspect of life. She was a tremendous example and force to the ones she mingled with on this earth, and she imparted on Stephen the opportunity to be open to the intangible and to share it with us. Stephen took this opportunity to go beyond; to be open to forces beyond himself and beyond his control and to search for answers, strength, and wisdom. I am honored to have had the opportunity to know Stephen, and to read his words."

~ Kim Kuhar, DO

(Reprinted by permission of Dr. Kim Kuhar)

Something More...an Introduction

Much of what is to follow will ask that you are willing to believe that there is something more to your life. It will, however, not ask you to give up thoughts, beliefs, and values that you already hold as truth. It is a message about awakening and remembering. It is not about needing more, but that there is something more. It is not about ourselves not being good enough, but rather about having more good for ourselves.

Let us liken ourselves to a crystal with many facets or faces. One face (the 'now self') looks, and lives, in this time and world of Earth. Even as we experience the Earth reality, we simultaneously live in many other worlds, or realities. Imagine the wonder of getting to meet or know our greater selves even as we live here now. At some time during our journey through life and space we will come to do this.

Ultimately this will become a most satisfying and grand discovery. So many of the fears, doubts, and questions will fall away into the splendor of knowing how it is that we are connected.

As the following words, verses, and experiences hope to awaken the something more within you, the message is also a declaration of our collective intention. We—all of us—with our vessel, planet Earth, have a destiny. There is intention and purpose in our presence in this time and place. Together we journey upon a great sea of living space. We are not an accident; but we may need to awaken in time in order to avoid one. Within us is the beginning, but hopefully not the end, of this incredible existence experience.

The events described in the pages ahead are real; however, in the interest of respecting the privacy of others, the names of some people and places have been changed.

1

"Javunda"—Another World

My first personal experience with this discovery occurred as a young child of four. It was a hot haymaking day in 1951 on the family farm in Gettysburg, PA. Riding on a tractor, stretching and peering ahead of the nasty hay bailer looking for any pheasants or rabbits that might be saved, I was grabbed by one of the large rear wheels, passed up on the rubber tire cleats, and carried down under the weight of the tractor. My final memory of this event was of my small fingers wrapping around the rubber cleat and saying, "Oh, No!"

As might be expected, witnesses to this accident (my father and older brothers) saw something like pizza sauce or Jell-O emerge from under the giant wheel. In later accounts Mom spoke about her pushing me together and lifting me up on her lap, where she cradled me, limp and rubbery, as Dad rushed the family Packard toward Gettysburg hospital. She spoke of something amazing happening at some point along this five-mile ride. My body firmed up in her lap and regained form and rigidity. For myself, I did not know. I was somewhere else; but obviously I also remained upon the Earth. From the moment the tractor's tonnage climbed over my body I was miraculously received into another realm—a place I understood to be Javunda. It was such a place, such a space, and such a land!

> It was such a place
> Where life lived
> And where death was not even known.

After what seemed to be forever, I understood that I was being "returned to sender". With a great deal of reluctance I was pushed back into my Earth's skin (so to speak), while simultaneously being pulled by my brothers' calling and the longing look upon my mother's face.

Following the "Oh, No!" my next conscious Earthly moment was when I opened my eyes and I saw my father and mother by my bedside with a brand new toy log truck. I came to be told that it had been four days since the accident, and that my parents had been trying to take me home since my arrival. I had been protesting vigorously against the hospital stay for the entire four days. During this time the doctors had not been able to find anything substantially wrong with me.

So, this farm experience introduced me to another world (reality) to which I also belonged. Even as I wind down my Earthly travels, I know I reside in this other world as well. During the 52 years that have elapsed since that day in the fields of Gettysburg I have returned to this world of Javunda a handful of times. Even early on as a young farm boy I had become aware that there was something more!

> Life need not always be firmed up.
> Much of it is fluid.

Perhaps it is in the fluid part of existence where most of the magic is, where the mystery lives, and the revelations are more likely to occur. In and during the experience of the tractor and other edge adventures (the blizzard, the falls, the bridge, the fast, the bees) I have come to know that the seeming death before us is also a door open for us. As painful as it may be getting to this door, there is something more—much, much more.

The lesson that there are different designs and laws for each world came from my mother, Virginia. When she would find me lying in the grass looking longingly into the nighttime skies, she would remind me that I was sent back for a reason, and even if it took the rest of my Earth life, I would one day understand why. She would say, "Stephen, come now, you must concentrate fully upon this world. Come into the house and live with your family." Years later, as I languished on a fast in Montgomery County Prison she sent me a book that most succinctly spoke to this: <u>Be Here Now</u>, by Richard Alpert.

Many of the thoughts, visions, and experiences that follow will speak to the importance of 'being here now' for all of us. *All hands on deck!* Something great and lasting is now in our hands. The success or failure of this entire existence experience—the 'Earth Reality'—may hang in the balance. Its very success shall soon depend on the collective weight of all life taken simultaneously.

As we continue along on this road to opportunity, understanding, and discovery it must be remembered that some of what will be expressed comes from places (spaces) where words cannot follow. In these instances we will do what humans do quite well when confronted with mystery and challenge—we will grope. Verse may be used to touch upon the impression intended. A stretch of the imagination may be equally as appropriate. Together we will lift the curtain and reconnect with the more of what we are, as well as the time when this journey began so many, many years ago in ages long gone by (but not forgotten).

> In the beginning we were sent forth
> There was nothing but darkness in the sea before us.
> Together we lifted the sails
> Upon the vessel of Earth.
> We would see this night through.
> We would sprinkle light (and life) into the vast darkness
> As we traveled across this great (but not endless) sea.

Traditional mental processes of cause and correlation can satisfy some of truth and knowing, but much more cannot be known in this way. As we share these words and impressions their value and validity may need to be measured by "How do they feel?" Do they create a vibration or reaction in you? Does something tingle? Does a long lost but not forgotten memory seem to have been perked?

Another condition of this journey or awakening into other worlds and realities may, at times, be a sense of loneliness. My subjective feeling, as I move into the end-run of my Earth life, is that nothing really sticks. There is no permanence. In fact, my entire 57 years feels like it has passed in the blink of an eye. It is so important to me to know that when I finally take leave of this beautiful world there is somewhere to go; in fact, a world where life will send a beginning but not an end.

The Return Home

> The call had gone out
> A great many beings were seen approaching in the distance
> A vocal murmur accompanied them
> As they moved forward in a cluster
> Toward an ever-narrowing causeway.
>
> A gentle mist lightly cloaked a small bridge
> That narrowed to single file.

Some among them hesitated and stepped aside.
A peaceable silence spoke to the magic
And momentousness in the air.

Steadily, though hesitantly, they stepped
One by one upon the bridge.
As they stepped upon this bridge
A veil of sorts was parted.
A long memory with a familiar recovery
Was beginning to awaken in them.

One by one they came
Knowing as they passed over this bridge
That there was no going back.
This was a one-way causeway.

As they stepped off the bridge
They had, in a few steps,
Crossed a great divide
And they knew!

The gentle mist upon the bridge now became a sweet and giving rain, washing tears from flowering faces, melting old clothes from their being. They stood naked but replenished under the bright sky of a new world. Familiar voices called out to them and came to take them in their arms. Newly come, they walked daintily upon the flowers under a sky with two suns. Celebration and merriment were all about. As they celebrated they were remembered for this great and long journey they had been on.

Now in this world
With the double sun
There was life returned
As it had begun.
Life would once again
To them send
A beginning without an end.

Even to this day it amazes me how an exceptional experience or heavenly type contact can leave us feeling so alone. In fact, it may be quite the nature of this existence experience that the hand can never completely close on anything. Separation and division constantly tear at attachment and love. Again, I credit my mother with sharing a great wisdom with me early on: "Stephen, do not get attached to the results. OK, live this life fully, but remember it may be taken away at any time. That's just the way it is."

When I returned from the hospital I felt as if I had so much to celebrate and share with my family. But no one (other than Mom) would allow me the intimacy we had before the tractor incident, nor did they care to hear about the other world.

> Perhaps it may have been easier for them
> Had I died instead
> Of returning home alive.

It may have been easier for their minds that way, instead of reconciling what they had seen with my return home seemingly well and alive. For some time I tried to reconnect with my brothers, but it seemed not to be. I remember being approached in the barnyard by my brothers and being probed by sharp sticks and having hard chunks of cattle dung lobbed at my head. At the time I thought they were envious of the shiny new log truck Dad had given me. Our father seldom gave a gift or a complement, and he was harsh in his discipline.

Soon, however, with my mother's comfort and guidance and the company of the many animals on the farm I was able to transfer my attachments to the cattle and the pigs. I became especially attached to "Pig the Wig". I would bring her table scraps and she would wait patiently for me in the corner of the pigpen, delivering quite a fuss over me each day upon my arrival.

When I entered my first year of school "Pig the Wig" would miss me, and I would miss her. At the end of the school day I would hurry up the ½ mile lane to hug her and kiss her. Then came a most hurtful day, one day early in the season of winter. There was a lazy snow falling when I reached the top of the drive and circled the John Deere shed. There was my friend "Pig the Wig", hooked in the rear hocks and hanging upside down, throat slit, and blood running to the ground. My father and uncle were butchering my good friend. Terror settled in me, as anger and loss overwhelmed me. Finding a soup can, I collected some of her blood and drank it from the can. With blood and tears falling to the ground I fled to the upper hayloft, telling my father that I hated him, and that I might have to kill him someday.

Mom soon found me there, crying up a storm. On this occasion she lent me the important and still valued wisdom, "Do not get attached to the results." Not only have these simple words of wisdom helped me as I've made my way through this world, I've also been able to refer to them to help others.

A few years ago I was called by a long-time friend. He had been out of touch for a while, and he asked me if I could meet him at the hospital. His father was dying and was having a very hard time letting go. When I arrived at the hospital I found his father (who I never really knew), surrounded by his family and stuck full of tubes from head to toe. He was gasping as he labored to breathe. I took his hand and sat down beside him, and I found him surprisingly lucid and coherent.

Soon I was asking him what he felt was next for him—what was awaiting his imminent departure—to which he responded, "Nothing". To this I gently spoke of the more of life, the wonder of the journey, and the everlasting nature of it all. About 40 minutes into our dialogue his breathing worsened, he dropped my hand, and he began moving his head back and forth. He was clearly agitated, and I was quickly moved into the hallway by two of his equally agitated daughters. At this point I was fiercely scolded for trying to "change" their father's beliefs. I could only respond that I hadn't come to <u>change</u> his beliefs, but to give him belief.

Sometime in the next couple weeks I received word from my friend informing me that his father had passed over. Upon hearing this news I again apologized for overwhelming him at the hospital. He responded that his father's last request was that I could return to see him. Being back in PA, I was too far away; still, I was greatly relieved that the power of the message may have helped this man let go of this world, and in doing may have allowed him to open a door to the next.

Nonetheless, there was something to be learned from the uncomfortable scene at the hospital:

> If we intend to comfort
> Then we must go gently
> If we take someone from the closet
>> To the window
> We must protect their eyes
> Remembering that light does not enter darkness

To destroy it or even replace it,
But rather to illume.

What was the message left with Mr. Davis? The nature of this journey and our place in it demands that we ride many horses, utilize different vehicles (i.e. our body). We must know that when this horse (body) is spent we have to let it go. Yes! Love this time, this world, this body, but don't become inseparably attached to it. New moments in the same or other meadows await us.

We have ridden under many suns as we have entered many dawns and then passed again through evening light to once again ride (journey) in the morning of yet another new day.

Do not allow that which is eternal for us to end here, clinging to a dying horse! Willingly trusting in the rhythm of nature and the renewal of life is the best means of continuing upon our journey and completing the hopes and promises of our parting so very long ago. We may not now remember, but we have not lost what matters—the eternal pulse of life!

The parting Mr. Davis:
"Am I worthy of this heaven-like place?
I shame for some of the things I have done."

About possible sin and mistakes made: These would belong to the long and difficult night that we journey through. As we continue on, mistakes made will remain with the world and reality, as will our bodies (horses, mounts, vehicles) in which they occurred. The soul of our being will best be guided by the illuminated light of creation, a light that has always shined upon us and will never forsake us. For our spiritual leanings it is important that we believe that we are of God and from God. We are not forgotten angels or souls to be tortured or enslaved to some karmic debt or original sin.

Judging by the way we are holding on to this world, we do not wish our identities to be lost or forgotten. Having faith in and trusting in the onward journey (that there is something more to life) is the best way to maintain a future and historic self. To be firmed up in eternal existence such that you might know yourself, see yourself, and feel yourself is implied in the completion of this journey. Should we fall and lose ourselves then we shall be returned to the all-amorphous vibratory pulse of life itself.

So please, Sir
Let go, be on your way.
For me the only thing to fear,
Is to be stuck here!

Do not allow your eyes to close upon this world without valuing your presence here. Quietly embrace the journey before you. Valuing the journey will excite and enflame the spirit wind, which will guide and carry you on.

For some time Mr. Davis had held on here, with a deficit of belief in his eternal nature. Why? Was it that he so loved this world that he could not bear to lose his eyes to it? Perhaps he celebrated the body-self as though it was the end-all of what we are all about, or want to be all about. Did he not, like so many of us do, seek to fashion a permanent home in a sometimes light, but often shadowy, and always fleeting world? In this scenario, faith and trust in our lasting nature and true value are jettisoned for the objective—touchable material kingdom that may attempt to throw a fence around us, as might a jailer's keeper. Or, like so many of us who have accumulated so much "stuff" and developed so much technology, have we over-valued this time and age?

If we are holding on here, are we withholding something special from ourselves? Can we be prodded gently with a message of something more? Can we be awakened from a purposeless sleep? In some cases we must be made aware of the stupor of self-indulgence often connected to our raft of accumulated "stuff". If we can be awakened then we may be reminded that we are upon a great and valuable journey. It is a journey of such great space-time and distance that we must remain fluid as we slip effectively from one mount to another!

Cheezer-Wheezer

2

Cheezer-Wheezer

Opening doors into other worlds enriches but may also complicate ones life. It is very difficult to focus on the everyday at times of these encounters. For me, there is no special formula for controlling the comings and goings of the essence, spirit, and sometimes the outline of these other-worldly beings. Stepping into other worlds or crossing into other realities implies some type of aperture—opening doors, raising windows, or parting curtains. On each occasion that we enter into another realm energy and beings may and sometimes will follow us back. The form and character of these otherworldly contacts may vary a great deal. The extent to which these contacts (essence—spirit—beings) appear and reveal their fluid or firm presence to us may depend largely upon what we are ready for, formed in part by our own perceptual eye and mental constructs, and how much we will allow ourselves to see or experience.

There are also times when realities cross (doors open) and our perceptions are purely accidental to our being at a certain place (space) and time. For me, I have met these beings in many different forms and degree of fluidity. Perhaps the most common contacts are the spirit or essence of beings from the unseen, which first appear as, concentrated points of light. I refer to them as 'tap-screws'. Tap screws glow with blue-green and sometimes red, and they can be hot to the touch. There is nothing quite so exhilarating as seeing these tap screws sprinkled from the sky, or meeting them at stream or woods edge as I enjoy an evening walk.

Another way I have characterized these beings, when they appear in a fluid type form with any number of shapes and sizes, is as 'spacers'. A characteristic of spacers is the curly-whirly fluidity from which they seem to emerge and to which they ultimately return. This curly-whirly form is a moving outline of something or somebody that is seldom clear or exactly defined. However, that something is going on is definitely clear.

> Something's shining
>> Is it kin?
> Somebody is knocking
>> At the door
> Something is coming in…

Spacers seem to most often appear first between objects such as boulders and trees, yet also seem capable of merging with them or passing through them, then reappearing on the opposite side. Even though they have recognizable form they are very fluid in nature. Spacers seem to recognize or feel one's gaze upon them, often shuffling away from a direct focus. If one relaxes his eyes and ears a clear perception of their form and sound often becomes available.

> Life need not always
>> Be firmed up
> Much of it is fluid!

Returning now to my days on the farm, allow me to introduce you to one of my most endearing and cherished friends of these early years—Cheezer-Wheezer. Cheezer-Wheezer was a character of characters, with both a humorous and nasty disposition. He was as often grumpy as he was friendly. You never knew in which mood you might find him. Cheezer-Wheezer inhabited a giant Pignut Hickory tree in the back woods along the northern property line. For reasons I will discuss later, trees are often the gatekeepers between worlds or realities. Trees are one of those exceptional living things that can cross over and live in two worlds at one time. As such, they sometimes seem to be a junction (connection) between here and there, where the unseen (Curley-Whirly) can melt, crossover, then solidify again (Spacer). In this process they seem to enter and leave trees as we would open and close our car doors.

I first met Cheezer-Wheezer during one of my cattle watches. I disliked working with the chickens, and had gladly taken on the role of herdsman as soon as I was big enough. I was responsible for moving the beef-cattle herd and their calves to distant, but unfenced, parts of the farm for summer grazing. I rose early each morning, took my stick, my dog Judy, and sometimes a sister or two, and headed off to my duties near the North Woods. Under one arm was a roughly tied pack containing a baked-bean sandwich and a mason jar full of ice water wrapped in newspaper—my sustenance for the duration of my cattle sitting. A ritual part of this daily expedition was the sharing of this meager lunch with my trusted companion, Judy. Together beneath the cooling canopy of a shade tree we would savor this gastronomic simplicity, and revel in our inter-species kinship.

It was along the footpath to this North meadow destination that the giant Hickory tree stood, proudly gracing the forest. Its roots firmly hugged the earth, while its limbs gently caressed the sky. It provided a perfect rest and respite place for both the cattle and me, and we often stopped there for them to graze and me to gaze. On one such hot day the cattle abruptly discontinued grazing and began moving toward the woods. I followed along with them. It was ever so much easier to allow them to lead me than to try to control 100 head of fly-bitten, thirsty cattle, especially since I was performing my task unassisted that day. Only if they had veered toward the 16-acre field of corn would I have pitched a fit on them and turned Judy loose upon their noses. The offense of allowing the cattle to consume the corn was as grievous as was the offense of losing cattle, and both were severe enough to warrant a session answering to Dad in the woodshed.

The cattle only wandered as far as the little stream near the woods edge, and as they waded in the water, drank lazily, and busied themselves with the flies, Judy and I sat back down under the large Hickory tree. After we partook of our bean sandwich and ice water, I skinned the bark off a small sapling and used the end product to tease a parade of black ants that were ascending and descending the trunk of the tree with deliberate precision and obvious purpose. I was pondering their mission when Judy suddenly yelped and ran off into the woods. I heard a thump close by, then felt the stinging thud of a falling hickory nut bouncing off my shoulder. I looked up in time to see another nut come whizzing past my head. I heard, "Cheeze-a-wheeze! Cheeze-a-wheeze!" and there he was. In the form of something between a squirrel and a midget gnome, he peered down at me from approximately 40' up in the tree and verbalized loudly before wiggling his furry body into the hollow of the old tree.

As I came to know Cheezer Wheezer he showed himself to be approximately the size of a woodchuck or a small dog. He had long forearms, short squat rear legs, a round head with beady eyes, and a wide mouth with black whiskers. His back feet appeared to have two or three toes, and his forelegs gave the impression of ending in full, furry hands.

At the time I thought nothing of what became so apparent later on—that he was a visitor from beyond. In retrospect I would identify Cheezer Wheezer as a spacer—a being from another world who was able to cross over from another space or reality using the Hickory tree as his juncture (gate/door/highway). I did, however, realize that he was an animal I had never seen before, and when I returned to the barn that evening I related my story to my father, and asked him what this creature might be. He listened to my story with uncharacteristic interest, shook his head, and told me that, although he didn't know what I might have seen, he would look into it himself the next morning.

The following day my father joined me as we moved the cattle out from the barn and toward the grazing field by the North Woods. That my father was joining me was a bit unusual, but of greater concern was the long-barreled 12-gauge shotgun he carried over his arm. How I feared for Cheezer Wheezer! When my father carried that gun something always died.

Although I was afraid to, I knew I had to lie. When we entered the woods I looked for another large Hickory tree to which I could direct my father's attention. Soon I found one some 100 feet from Cheezer Wheezer's tree. It was a very tall, but not so wide and high Hickory tree. In its crown was a copious nest—perhaps that of a squirrel or even a hawk. Without so much as a word my father pulled up the long barrel and shot into the nest. A family of squirrels sprang from the nest and raced out the small branches that served as their highway system to the crowns of adjoining trees. One unfortunate furry fellow tumbled to the ground, dead. Picking it up by the tail my father noted that there wasn't enough meat on this squirrel for anything but stew. He then asserted that all that I had seen was a very large squirrel, and that the nuts that I thought were thrown at me were accidentally dropped by the somewhat clumsy younger members of the squirrel clan. The sound, he said, was a sound he had never heard of before; and that, along with the size and caricature of what I thought I saw was something that happens to boys when they are alone in the woods. Whew!

It was difficult chewing and swallowing the thick bowl of stew that evening; but I was inwardly happy that it wasn't Cheezer Wheezer we were dining on! I couldn't sleep that night as I waited eagerly to return to the woods and listen again for that sound, "Cheeze-a-wheeze! Cheeze-a-wheeze!"

Father

Carroll Redding

Eventually I would involve my mother in the secret of my friend Cheezer Wheezer. After a few visits into the woods he revealed himself to her. She never did actually see him, but she could clearly hear his voice and, as she noted, his laughter. How compelling this furry, gnome-like visitor became for us. My Weimeraner, Judy, was equally attracted to Cheezer Wheezer and his comings and goings from the beyond. How she perceived Cheezer Wheezer I'm not sure; but clearly she was interested and after we made our acquaintance with Cheezer Wheezer she made many solo trips from the farm to the North Woods. She did, however, keep a safe distance from the Hickory tree—always taking a patient position some 60'-70' from its base.

Cheezer Wheezer only showed himself once every 5 or 6 weeks, and then it was only after I waited for an hour or two by the special tree. On one occasion while we waited for Cheezer Wheezer to reveal himself, I asked Mom how Cheezer Wheezer appeared to her. She seemed to see a curly whirly outline form of this character, but never saw him clearly defined as I did. "But Mom," I asked, "Why do you not see exactly what I see?" My mother reassured me as she taught me this: "Stephen, the things you and I may see and experience may be things that others cannot see." Cannot see?? "And if they are not ready to see they may respond with fear, and fearful people may be hurtful people." (ie. my father with his long gun.) "If they are ready to see they will see. And if not, you cannot force them to see." She observed that Cheezer Wheezer was "an old, capable, and important spirit." His almost constant chatter she heard quite well. Closing her eyes and resting her head against an adjoining tree she seemed to drink intensely of his moody ramblings. Such an experience could put a smile on her face for days. On days when Cheezer Wheezer did not make an appearance my mother would teach me about life as we thoroughly enjoyed the woods with its songs of the birds, blooms of the wild flowers, fragrance of the Sassafras, and fresh berries on the bushes. Even on those days we would linger a little longer, making one last pass by the big Hickory tree, hoping to once again be awed by the presence of this distant traveler who had taken up residence in our woods.

Over the next couple of years Mom and I made frequent trips into the North Woods. If we weren't grazing the cattle we were picking blackberries or mushrooms. At times we encouraged the whole family to come along for a Sunday picnic. Each time we passed by his tree we listened for that now-familiar "Cheeze-a-wheeze" sound. At times Mom felt that there was more than one other worldly being in the Hickory habitat. Perhaps the entire Cheezer-Wheezer family had crossed over for a visit to the North Woods on the Redding family farm on the planet Earth.

Witchie-Willie

3

Witchie-Willie

With Mom's help, love, and guidance I got past the Pig-the-Wig tragedy. Instead of trying to reaffirm the relationships with my older brothers I connected happily with two younger brothers and a younger sister. They were siblings number 6, 7, & 8 (I was #5) of what would eventually be a total of 15 children. Joy in living once again returned to me in the everyday play and work on the farm. These younger family members had not been born yet at the time of the accident, and they seemed to like me just fine. During one phase of motherhood my mother brought forth six girls in a row. Life became so much fun again. What I lacked in my relationships with my older brothers was more than compensated for by my kinship with my sisters.

I did, however, honor my mother's lead, and spoke little of the miracle in the hay field. When it did come up I passed over it as quickly and quietly as possible. I did enjoy instigating some interest in the matter by teasing my sisters' imaginations with, "Hey, girls, can you imagine if we knew of another world, and we could live there also?" The subject never failed to draw intent listening. Even then people had an appetite for this something more! Many of us, I believe, have recognition on some level of other faces in other places. I think that perhaps our minds, as well as our souls, have historic contact with the past. After tickling their interest I might catch myself, remembering not to "shed a light too brightly upon sleeping children's eyes." Invariably my sisters or friends might ask, "Where are you reading this stuff?" Or they might simply comment, "What an imagination you have!"

During these years the intimacy and trust between Mother and myself continued to grow. Sadly, however, since the bloodletting of Pig-the-Wig the great distance from Dad would just never quite mend.

Along with herding the cattle, I continued to sharpen my skills and understanding of the wonderful process of calving. I had 80+ head of beef cattle and one or two bulls in my care. For major issues of injury, difficult birthing, or barn or fence repair my older brothers and father would step in as needed, but at the young age of 8 to 10 years old I became the cattleman, responsible for the winter feeding, bedding, and general oversight of the herd. The barn became my mansion. Oh, how the great timbers would creak in high wind, and what a soothing sound the rain would make when it fell on the black tin roof! My ruminary friends and my dog Judy were my constant companions, confirming daily my feelings of value and being needed.

Along with tending the larger herd, it was also my duty to hand milk a few dairy cows for the family milk supply. My favorite cow of all time, "Blacky", was one of these 'milkers'. To this day I can still smell the aroma of that sweet, foamy milk rising in a stainless steel bucket, as I rested my head in Blacky's rear flank and pulled on her udder.

It was here in the barn where I entertained myself on the backs of adolescent cows. They were big and strong enough to carry me as I slid from the hayloft above onto their backs, yet they were young enough to revel in the play without real aggression or fear. No sooner did I seat myself on the unsuspecting calf's back than the rodeo was on, with a steady chorus of kicking and jumping until I unceremoniously landed at their feet in the bedding. On rare occasions I was lucky enough to get an extended ride out of the barn and into the meadow before I was heaved off their backs onto the uneven ground.

Being mindful of my mother's advice about attachment that followed the Pig-the-Wig disaster, I was able to just enjoy the farm while allowing room for adventure almost every day. Then along came "Pluto" and "Sparta". These were two black and white spotted calves that were weaned early from a large Holstein cow Dad had purchased to use for family milk. These two calves had a special air about them, and a unique relationship developed between them and me. It is amazing how love and attachment can sneak up on you. In one hour it's just an ordinary thing; but in the next hour something unseen, but powerful and extraordinary has happened. It is almost as if the boundaries of something important outside of you has melted at the same time a part of you has also melted, and the two separate beings flow together in an inseparable way. Together this fluid like vibration—heart and soul—is inseparable from itself, and a deep sense of caring and interest bubbles up from a magical place in us. Once this we-ness begins we are somehow bigger than we were even an hour earlier. Windows to the self are opened; unknown locks are loosed. Something so very important flowers within and around us.

And for this time, at least
We are part
Of the secret of the bloom.

These two four-footers received special treatment indeed. Dad bought two feeding buckets with 5"x2" nipples from which they drank their substitute milk.

At first they showed little interest in the milk-powder substitute, and they cried long into the night. I cried also. Soon I found myself diverting some of their mother Daisy's milk and some of Blacky's milk into their customized feeding buckets. It seemed so harsh that they should be taken from their mother so soon! I did my best to calm them, bed them, and pet them in their own special shed.

Once again I found myself rushing up the ½ mile long lane after school so I could be with them. As soon as the large herd was fed and bedded, off I would go to their shed. I loved to pet and groom their curly cow hair. In return they would extend their large orangey-yellow hairy tongues and drag their sticky saliva over my face and head until my cheeks looked winter-burned.

Soon Sparta and Pluto were big enough to carry me, and off into the meadow we would ride. When one got exhausted I would dismount (fall off), and without hesitation pop up onto the back of the other. We made an unusual and unlikely trio, and our excursions had all the earmarks of three youthful friends having fun.

One year early summer found me in the far meadows of the farm overseeing the cattle herd. Pluto and Sparta had joined the larger herd. They were off the substitute milk and could graze and chew their cud very well indeed. By mid-morning or so the herd was collected together and was busy grazing a safe distance away from the corn. The cornfields were always a critical factor in cattle grazing. If the cattle got into the corn, not only would they ruin a valuable crop, but if they ate more than a few stalks they would become bloated and deathly ill. Gasses from the corn would expand their stomachs until the tissue was stretched like a drum. This hugely expanded stomach would interfere with their breathing, and ultimately shut down their lungs. A very large percentage of bloated cattle eventually die. I once saw our neighbor, farmer Witherow, stick an ice pick into 8-10 prized dairy cows who were suffering from this malady. These cows were on their sides, tongues extended, with eyes rolled back in their heads. Farmer Witherow moved quickly among them, sticking each in it's great bloated stomach, then pressing their sides to expel as much gas as possible—s-w-i-s-h-s-h-s-h, like the air escaping from an old tire. Although this technique temporarily relieved the pain (both the cows' and Farmer Witherow's), it proved not to be a solution. A few hours after this barnyard emergency-room episode the cows were all standing and appeared normal. One by one, however, over the next ten days these precious bovines succumbed to infections caused by their life-saving stab wounds. Eventually all but one perished.

On our own farm I witnessed David and Dad attempting unsuccessfully to relieve the bloat by inserting a rubber hose down the esophagus in an effort to relieve the gas. There did not seem to be a farm cure for this condition.

On this day in the field, with everything seeming under control, I briefly trusted that all would be well if Judy and I ran into the adjacent woods to look in on our cantankerous friend Cheezer Wheezer. We found him busy at the base of his Pignut Hickory tree, all but caught off guard by Judy's sudden approach as she ran up for a brief sniff of this strange little critter. Instantly Cheezer Weezer slipped into the tree, through a door I could never find. Soon he reappeared on his normal limb just outside a large cavity in the upper canopy. On this occasion Cheezer Wheezer was absolutely entertaining. I imagined that he was happy not to have been nibbled or otherwise assaulted by the infamous sniffing Weimeraner. Whatever the cause, he was graceful in this jig-like dance and more full of chatter than ever before. Soon I was lying on my back with my head on Judy's belly, gazing at the antics in the tree above.

Suddenly I heard the rustle of hooves in the woods. The cattle were coming in for water and shade. Oh, my God, I had left them for hours! Frantically I ran back to the grazing area to see if all cattle and calves were accounted for. As my eyes swept across the grassland and back to the woods, my gaze stopped as I noted something on the ground over by the corn field. Help! It was little Sparta lying there bloated, with corn fodder still in her mouth. I ran up to her and cried for her to get up. Already her eyes were rolled back and her belly was taught as a drum. She was almost done!

Instantly I knew I had to break all the rules, and to Witchie Willy's house I ran. Past the cornfield, through the brambles, and over an old woven fence I continued, pushed onward by the urgency of my mission. Finally I crossed the stream with no water in it, ran up the embankment, and crashed against her rickety cabin door. I looked Witchie Willie right in her little magical eyes, even as Joe the Crow screamed and pecked at Judy's head. I was not deterred! If there was ever any magic in that large steaming kettle that always sat upon her wood-burning stove, we needed it now. There would be time to review protocol later. "Witchie Willie, Witchie Willie," I panted, "Sparta is down! I need you now! I need you <u>now</u>!!"

Without even taking a moment to question why (she seemed to know), she ladled out some brew into an old soda bottle. It was a smelly green concoction with a lumpy texture and a consistency best described as gunky. I am certain to this day that nobody in this world or any other knew what was in that brew except for Witchie Willie herself.

It was amazing how fast Witchie Willie was. Her bony old body was clad in layers of winter-like clothes in the middle of summer. Still, she moved almost effortlessly over the fence and through the stickers, along the edge of the cornfield where we found Sparta. She looked dead. She was not moving; I could see no sign of breathing, no fluttering of her eyelids, no movement in the tip of her tail. My heart ached at the sight, and my body stood paralyzed with fear and disbelief at the sudden, hideous apparent demise of my friend.

"Boy! Lift her silly head!" The crackling, cranky voice cut through my flood of overwhelming emotions and numbly I hurried to comply. As I struggled to lift Sparta's head, Witchie Willie quickly stuck the neck of the soda bottle down her throat. Gurgle, gurgle, gurgle. The brew was released. Soon a discharge even more disgusting than Witchie Willie's brew erupted from Sparta's mouth, along with the deftly applied green goo.

"Now lift the animal up, Boy, up onto her silly feet." She always called me "Boy", as if not calling me by name helped insure that she would never risk my thinking that she felt any closeness or affection toward me whatsoever. With heroic effort I struggled with Sparta, pulling by tail and by ear until she was up. Gas of incredible stench poured from her, and her eyes slowly set back into their proper sockets. Sparta would live this day through, and would continue to live along with the herd. My friend made it; and my butt was spared Dad's razor strap, which surely would have awaited me in the woodshed if the outcome had been different. What could have been a time of tragedy instead became a day of miracles, and I was happy, grateful, and newly aware of the seriousness of my responsibilities, as well as the joy of doing each day's tasks to the best of my ability. There would be no more moments of lapsed attention for me while I tended my herd!

For one infinitesimal moment I thought I saw an expression of satisfaction cross her craggy face. Then, without so much as a brief "Goodbye", Witchie Willie turned and began the hike back toward her cabin. This was as much emotion as I would ever see in her intensely private, stone-cold countenance.

Witchie Willie first peaked the interest of this farm boy when, one day while perched in a tree in the deep woods, I looked over past the corn field and caught a glimpse of a wisp of smoke rising from an area I heretofore thought was uninhabited. From this vantage point I could make out the crooked roof line and the leaning chimney of Witchie Willie's cabin. I was intrigued, curious, and mesmerized by the prospect of this mysterious inhabitant; yet I was also timid, and intensely aware of the #1 rule on the farm—"you must never leave the property." Never being hesitant to pursue the absolute boundaries of the rules on the farm, in subsequent days I slowly worked my way toward this vagabond's plantation. Not that it was a great distance away. It was maybe ½ mile at the most, although the thick cover of brush and sticker bushes that made up our back property line was a formidable barrier to my travels. Once we had blazed our initial trail, it would still take Judy and me 2 hours to get there, and if we stayed to "spy" a little, we would end up using the better part of our day for this adventure.

In contrast to my other "secrets" that I shared with my mother, this was one secret I had to keep only unto myself. As much as I would have liked to share this incredible tale, the rule about not leaving the farm was ironclad and enforced by both parents. The risk of revealing this breach of our family contract was simply too great. Even more important in my mind was that I never wanted to put my mother in a position of being "in the middle" between me and my Dad. If he were ever to find out that I had broken the rule and that my mother knew about it and did nothing, the resultant fight would be catastrophic. There was more than one occasion when my behavior resulted in arguments late into the night, with my father voice rising, audible even at the second floor bedroom level. "I don't give a damn!" he would shout, "That kid has gotten between us. We've got to straighten him out!" My father was normally reserved and undemonstrative, but when he was angry he could be very mean, and my mother was usually on the receiving end of his misplaced cruelty.

So I kept my secret, and was as discreet as possible regarding my interest in and visits to Witchie Willie's house. No one needed to tell me that she was a witch. That fact was clear to see. Reflecting back, on one occasion when she did speak to me, she told me her name. She probably said her name was Millie, but all I heard was "Witchie Willie". She caught me spying and snuck up behind me, grabbing me by the neck. I could feel her substantial nails making indentations in my skin as she demanded to know who I was. "I'm a Redding boy," I stammered, "P-l-e-a-s-e don't tell my father I was here!" "Are you a witch?" I asked. "My name is Millie…" she answered. "Glad to meet you, Witchie Willie," I breathlessly replied, and from that moment forward the name stuck. "Boy, are you the one that was run over by the tractor some years back?" she asked. I nodded in reply. "Come in and set a spell," she demanded, "and have something to drink."

Well, I already knew about witches and what they could do to children. I had heard about spells and potions, and other mystical things. After all, wasn't her pet crow, Joe, some unfortunate soul who was now under her control? Clearly the crow was somehow indebted to her. She would throw scraps out the door to him, and he would spy for her. Sometimes he would disappear for hours, then return with pretty feathers or shiny papers that she would weave into pictures on her wall. Then there was her cauldron. I was mightily intrigued by her ever-simmering kettle. I even thought I saw her putting frogs, toads, and small bones into the brew, though I couldn't be certain since my view was through an old wavy glass window that was amply obscured by dirt and cobwebs.

Such an intriguing, frightening lady she was! Her aloneness and mystery were as thick as the humid Gettysburg summer air. And her appearance was so true to the myth of the witch. She looked older than old, all skin and bone. She had a tall head, a long beak of a nose, and small powerful eyes that seemed to crawl over your skin as she looked at you. Her exaggerated, pointed chin came way down below her thin-lipped crooked mouth, and the position of her wrinkles revealed the truth that this wizened old lady hadn't cracked a smile in years. Her face was ageless, her countenance sad. Though she kindled fear in me, I was simultaneously hopelessly drawn to her.

As time has passed I have come to a better understanding of the comings and goings of life's beings. I recognize now that Witchie Willie was one of those beings that could not completely die. She was not allowed to pass through the door! It was not that she was afraid of death. It was just that death would not come for her. Perhaps at one time she had misused her power. Perhaps she had never loved. Whatever the obstacle to moving on from this place, she would be here always, alone and alienated for this time.

> She would live and live
> Suffer and suffer
> And wield her magic alone.

Just as I was interested in her, she was interested in me. "How did you live, Boy? Answer me that. Everyone thought you were a goner, Boy. I'm sure you know that. Some say the hard earth opened up for you and not a bone in your body was broken. Yes, Boy?? No Boy?? Don't just sit there watching my stew, Boy!"

Though I was breaking my mother's rule being off the property, I did not forget her guidance. "Tell no one of this other world. It cannot help, it can only hurt you. The most they need to know is that the angels came for you!"

I should not have been surprised when Witchie Willie did not buy the angels story. "Angels! Angels!" she cackled, "Poppy-cock! They've never come for me,

Boy. Why should they come for you?" My weakly stammered explanation that she had never been run over as I had further soured the mood of the hag, and with a sweep of her bony hand she commanded, 'You'd better get on home now, Boy. And if you know what's good for ya' you won't be comin' round here no more." I did take my leave that day, but there was no way I could honor her request to stay away. I was attached to Witchie Willie, enamored by her magic, and intrigued by her power, and the depth of her sadness.

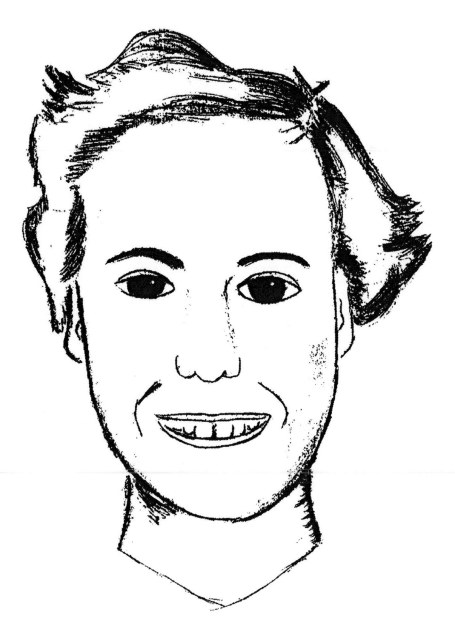

Mother

Virginia Bly Redding

4

Virginia's Gone

Often while falling asleep at night—almost ritual in delight—my siblings and I would entertain one another in story telling and conversation. As many as five or six of us would "cracker up" (snug together, all facing the same direction so our body contours interlocked in a human mosaic) under any number of army blankets. There, above our row of talking and laughing heads, our breath would rise, clearly visible in the frosty air. Winters were long and cold in the 1950's on the farm. With little heat in the house, and none upstairs in the bedrooms, it was easy to entice and capture willing listeners and snugglers and envelope them in a collective story telling until, one by one, we nodded off to sleep.

> Frost covered the single windowpanes
> The wind blew; the windows rattled
> And winter entered in.

When it came to be my turn to speak to or entertain the group in the bed, I would often use Witchie Willie as a subject and basis of my stories. I would never speak about the old lady beyond the far woods directly—that would definitely blow my cover and expose my traversing the boundaries of the farm. Among the Redding children no one could fathom committing such a crime! Nevertheless I incorporated her habits and behaviors into my stories, and the mental vision of Witchie Willie my siblings conjured up never failed to enrapture them. As our breath mixed with the opaque light of the moon and stars passing through the frosted windows the atmosphere of magic spells and devious powers seemed easy to convey.

> Fear and trepidation
> Seemed to rise above the bed
> Questions were asked and answered.

More stories were told
Until, at last, sleep surrounded our heads.

These times, though as fresh to me as yesterday, have long since passed, and I often ask, "Where has all the wonder gone?" The magic and mystery so central to our youth seems to be something far away and long forgotten in today's world. Is there not still a place for the wonder that can exercise our imaginations and nudge loose the doors to the unseen? Exercising these subjective faculties is inclined to keep us in touch with ourselves, which will encourage us to live our lives from the inside out.

Contrary to this, so many of us seem content to live on the surface of life, caught up with the 'bottom line', living our lives from the outside in. How have so many traded the top line (where we are in control of everything that matters to us) for the bottom line (where we are in control of nothing except the accumulation and distribution of monies and stuff?) The result of this ill-advised barter is that our precious lives are busied accumulating stuff and gaining relative power in our attempt to fill an emptiness within us. Whatever happiness or satisfaction we find along the way is short-lived and episodic, and we find that our state of being is often dependent upon someone else's folly. Their dance may not be our dance. When our satisfaction is dependent upon the outcome of political elections, stock market trends, sporting events, and the like we are, in essence, living at a gaming table in a bottom line casino. When living for the top line we ask ourselves what really matters to us. Inner peace and contentedness are our most sought-after rewards, and we find ourselves living in the intimacy of our own home, in the company of our heart and soul. So much of reaching our collective destiny—successfully completing this wondrous journey—will depend upon our ability to awaken from this bottom-line stupor and return to acknowledging the value of our inner being, as we return to the top-line of our lives.

Living our lives from the outside in
Slowly loses our soul
For its breath
We must live our lives
From the inside out.

How we have lived our life becomes so important toward the end of our life—in Earth time, that is. For those who have lived their lives from the outside in, thoughts or reflections of death are something to be avoided. In their final days the thought of dying elicits great fear, and all kinds of extraordinary means may be undertaken to extend the time of this life just a little bit longer.

Those who have practiced living from the inside out seem not so afraid in their final hours, and may, at times, even welcome death. These people seem to feel that they have lived their lives fully, and letting go at the end is not so impossible to do.

> As difficult as it may be
> To say good bye
> They see it as a door
> Through which they will
> Continue to fly.

Now when thinking of Witchie Willie I am certain that, even with all of her personal power, long life, and independence, her life was a lonely and often miserable experience. The last time I went to check on her was during my early college years. As I crossed the crest of earth that always served as the final threshold before her cabin came into full view, I was stunned to see a mysteriously changed landscape. All that was left of the ramshackle cabin that had so captured my curiosity as a youth was a faint outline of the four outside walls still visible on the ground and a small patch of firmly packed earth where her narrow footpath met the doorway of the cabin. I was dumbstruck by the reality that confronted me. The old woman who had seemed so timeless was no longer there. I spotted a woman on a horse in the next field. She appeared to be hunting, but when she saw me signal to her she steered her mount in my direction and met me half way. When I asked her about the 'Old Lady' she matter-of-factly stated that she was glad that somebody had finally "burned that old witch out". She said everybody knew that witch was "up to no good," and she added that she suspected that Witchie Willie might have been stealing her dogs and cats. Whew! When I asked about Witchie Willie's safety she replied, "They never did find her body."

> Of course not—
> She couldn't live…
> And
> She couldn't die…

I suspect she now resides in the unseen ethers somewhere or somehow. I also suspect that I will someday recognize her very distinguishable voice coming out of the shadows somewhere. She will be lonely, for sure, but not alone, as she has joined countless other disembodied spirits who are unable to find their way out of here.

> Tending too little with their lives
> Something else has not allowed
> For them there is no door
> And even if they were to shout
> There simply is no way out!

I fear for so many who walk upon the Earth today. The future abode may be more of a ghost town than a living garden! It is so essential that we be about living our lives from the inside out. Trusting our intuitive self and celebrating our being-ness will allow us to better know our greater selves. Even if we don't awaken to all the faces of our crystal self in this world, we can easily enough reclaim them when we move on. Not only will the value of our greater being be felt, the connectedness of our personal history will be more easily discovered. That will help us to know better what lies before us. The choice here is to live in the many rooms of our personal mansion, rather than in just one.

> …Let us not
> Close our shutters and pull our blinds
> Or darkness may all surround.
> The wax of this world
> Will eventually burn through…
> Even with borrowed candles
> We won't know what to do.

It is amazing the difference when love and compassion (the top line) are integrated into our lives. The powers of Witchie Willie were similar to those of my mother. Their energies were so compelling! The difference lay in the delivery, the countenance, the basic trust in the world in which they lived.

Mom was clearly a gifted one. A mother, of course, is gift enough, but she was something special. This was most evident to me when I viewed her from a distance. I would be utterly amazed to watch her with the chickens, especially on the range. The range is the open meadow stage of old-fashioned chicken raising. This is the pullet stage, before the chickens are reliable egg-a-day producers, when the young lady chickens were allowed in the meadows in the daytime and stayed in protective "range shelters" at night. Their diets consisted of grass, seeds, and insects, and a daily portion of "mash", which is a homogenized combination of corn, oats, molasses, etc. Feeding of this mash was done from a bucket once or twice a day, and whoever carried that bucket received a great deal of attention, indeed. Hundreds of these young hens would flutter and fly about the courier trying to be the first partaker of the mash distribution.

It was not unusual to see Mom walking among the pullets as we would feed them, but, surprisingly, even when she didn't have the bucket the hens would line up behind her and follow where she walked. Her presence was compelling even to a bunch of simple chickens.

There were many other instances of her quiet power and compelling nature, earning her a special status in my eyes and in the eyes of others. As children one of our favorite things was to follow Mom as she walked over the meadows and through the woods. Not unlike the chickens we would gather around her, fighting for a chance to hold her hand or gain her attention. Song sparrows would encircle her head, and wild flowers seemed to spring up at her feet. Diving to the ground, we would pluck the spring beauties to present to her. She would gently scold us for pulling them from the ground, saying:

"Each flower is a living thing.
Each one might dress a fairy queen."

But pull them we would, and she held our bouquet like a treasure. I couldn't help but wonder, were those flowers there before? Or had they sprung up from the ground as we walked to say hello to a special being on her way? As an adult today, with the understanding of what it takes to run a household and raise a family, I have no idea how she did all that she did. She tended to the animals, the house, and the children. She washed all of our clothes in an old-fashioned wringer washer. I would often hear it running late into the night—swish, swish, while the smell of the next day's bread baking wafted across our sleepy faces. Her special-ness was all around her home and family, and it touched everything she did and everyone she new. But, as often is true with truly exceptional people, she never seemed to notice her own special gift.

Although there is much to remember and celebrate about the way she lived, at this juncture the message I would like to convey concerns the way she died. Throughout her life Virginia had mastered the skills of natural healing. Early on it was more of a necessity than an art form. She had 15 children, 10 cats, 4 dogs, 10,000 chickens, 100+ cattle, assorted horses, pigs, and other livestock, each with its own specific individual needs, and at one time or another she helped them all, often achieving unbelievable results. Once during my graduate studies at an urban university I invited my friend Justin and his lady Carol to visit my family on the farm. On the second day of our visit Justin came quickly into the house, pleading with my mother for our family physician's number. Carol was fevered and in severe pain, cramping and bleeding, and unable to walk. Justin's jaw dropped when Mom replied, "Why, Justin, we don't have a family doctor." "Oh my God," was his memorable response, "you have 15 kids and you don't even have a doctor!" "Where is Carol?" Mom asked gently, with a calming, soothing tone. Some hours later, following some comfrey compresses, hands on treatment, and Cedron tea, Carol was resting comfortably, and the following day she was enjoying a family dinner with the entire Redding clan. Not that Virginia shunned modern medicine; in fact, in some instances she regarded it quite favorably. But her first choice was always to utilize natural healing applications with positive spiritual overtones, and her results were often most amazing.

As time passed, the rigors of the farm were assumed more and more by the children. Mom found it possible to visit Ghana in Central Africa and the Ama-zon River basin in South America. Following her contacts with unspoiled native cultures, Mom grew even more convinced of the healing power of herbs and spirit. Her own personal hybrid healing system was used extensively by her in her later years, and people came from far and wide to visit with the chicken farmer. One time a stranger came, and he sat with my mother and sisters drinking tea and conversing for about an hour before he asked Virginia when he might see her mother. Mom explained that her mother had passed away two decades earlier, to which the stranger insisted there had to be some mistake. He said he had come all the way from Alabama in the hopes of meeting with Mrs. Redding. The youth and general vitality that exuded from my mother's countenance had caused this stranger to assume that she and my sisters were of the same generation! With his misconception clarified, the visitor apologized and was again content to sip mint tea. He had met the healer, and you could see the contentment in his eyes.

The very best of her natural healing took place late in her life while residing in her final residence. Located in Hunterstown, PA, just down the road from Gettysburg, this was a home that had also been the home of her youth. In her later years she moved back there, leaving the family farm in the care of my oldest brother and his family. There are endless anecdotes about her skill and affinity for healing, but for now we are going to divert our attention from her life to her death. It is important to understand her end—her Earth-end, that is.

One fitful night I had a dream in which Mom's hand was outstretched to me as she receded into the mist. She was wearing the nightgown she wore on the morning of my father's funeral a few years earlier. In her other hand she had a clump of Cedron, a lemon-smelling herb I had smuggled from Peru to help her in her work. This dream was difficult. I wanted not this dream! I knew its validity though; one way or the other Mom would be leaving soon.

A dream can be such a potentially guiding hand. It can tell us so very much. The minds of the beings in this existence experience need to cultivate and trust their dreams. We must learn to feel what they mean. Dreams can be wonderful, fluid highways to our past and future presence—lines of communication and signals beyond the veil, from loved ones both sick and well.

Dreams:
Highways to the past and the
Future present
Lines of communication and signals
Beyond the veil
From loved ones in and out of this world
Both sick and well.

It was two days later when I received the call from Gettysburg. Mom had finished her daily jog and was not feeling well. My sister insisted upon taking

Mother to the hospital. She was diagnosed with thyroid cancer. A tumor was present, and surgery was imminently necessary. It couldn't be! Mom! So young—just 63 years old; so healthy; such a healer. It was!

True to her beliefs she would not run from death, but rather chose to embrace it. She would not accept radiation or chemotherapy (which may or may not have extended her life). This so angered her older children. They were not ready to let her go. Who was?

I so admired her for her courage in her final days. She was dying as she had lived—simply and completely prepared. "Simplify, simplify, simplify," was her final message to us as a family as we gathered around her bed. She sipped as she could on her herbal teas. She loved and suffered in her final days. I may have been her only clear and decisive get-going support as she slid slowly away. "Mom, let it go. It is time to be quickly on your way." Because of this, my sister saw me as somewhat responsible for Mom's disinterest in medical intervention, and thus not using my voice to encourage her to stay longer.

> But my mother knew how it was and is
> She came, and completely
> This life she lived!

Our last visit together came on a day in early May. Though her voice was faded and her speech slowed, her guttural request was clear as a bell to me. "Stephen, take me to the window; perchance I can see an oriole." Orioles were her favorite birds. Though orioles ordinarily roosted high, and I doubted that we could see one from the vantage point available in the kitchen, I lifted her wasted, bony body from the bed as my sister screamed at me to put her down. "Enough!" I said, as we made our way to the kitchen window. There, on the lowest branch of a Maple tree sat, and sang, a beautiful lone oriole. What a sight it was to see! And in the orange and yellow feathers of the underbelly, Mom's rising and setting sun signaled. Her forwarding call was finally given. Upon the oriole's melodic sound she flew away from here into the great sea.

Our Mother

> *The Spring song of the oriole is sung*
> *Your journey now continues into the sun*
> *So you have gone to there from here*
> *Our love for you will keep you near.*

Fifteen sailors you set upon the sea
　　In hope and trust their spirits would be set free.
Fourteen remain as we search the same
　　To give our lives meaning and love in your name.
Your sun rose in the East; it is now in the West
　　Your bearings have set our direction best.
Our hearts are now troubled by your passing,
　　This pain, our love, may it be everlasting!

"Melix"

From his world into our own
He crossed the great sea of night!

5

<u>Communion with Melix</u>

Some years have now passed since the passing of my mother, yet her support and affirmation of my personal connectedness to other worlds, other realities, continues to guide me. Though I am sure that she, too, drew from the well of the 'something more', her personal and first-handed experiences with the unseen and the beyond were frustratingly limited for her. She never tired of our conversations regarding Javunda—the many worlds to which we belong and the great journey we are upon.

> Creation set forth into the night
> Upon the vessel of Earth
> We would carry life's light
> Voyaging across the great sea of night.

Clearly Mom did her life completely. She stood strongly and honestly upon life's deck. She met each dawn with enthusiasm, continuing without reluctance to serve the ordinary and everyday quite well. It was apparent she was an enlightened and capable chicken farmer. She was a kind and compassionate mother of 15 children: David, Virginia, Michael, Riley, Myself (Stephen), Joseph, Sally, Loring, Kathleen, Cindy, Debbie, Phyllis, Peggy, Sharon, and Matthew. In her later years, my mother developed an accomplished sense of balance with natural healing that was delivered as an art, and that to many felt like a blessing. Still, her deeper being yearned to better grasp and know more completely the other faces of herself, along with a peek or two into the world into which we journey.

> That she might be
> Carried by this lovely Earth
> Into those protected harbors
> And step into that One-Day

With a beginning
But not an end.

Yes, she witnessed some of the incredible circumstances and recoveries of my edge experiences. "Stephen, I have no doubt about the things you see and believe. I wish more of us could see them and experience them with you."

In my company over the course of our togetherness there were a few peeks for her. One night I milked "Blacky" in the meadow, and a shaft of light burnt the Earth around us, leaving an undeniable glow and presence. How she celebrated when we walked and she saw and was acknowledged by a "tap screw" (a spirit being upon the Earth dressed in its glow)! And when the Christmas wren passed through the window! And on one occasion on a cloudy, overcast night when Javunda's beckoning light seemingly danced over the wood line on the Western horizon.

Clearly some special light
Had come some great distance
Through this cloudy night
Suspended there in Grace
~ and Delight!

As I reflect upon my mother's life I feel the embodiment of her presence was a message that could heal so many of us today—heal us from the inside out, reintroducing value and joy into our lives. I will never forget how completely and thoroughly she did her everyday chores: cleaning the floors, washing the clothes, baking the bread, caring for her children, overseeing the chickens, and much, much more.

On one occasion, when I was approximately 10 years old I remember her washing drinking glasses at the kitchen sink. I was impatiently waiting for her to finish this chore so we could go out into the yard to pick Spring Dandelions for a dinner dish. I was irritated at the extent to which she cleaned, then rubbed her fingers over the glasses until she was satisfied with the way they would squeak under the pressure of her fingers. "Mom," I asked, "Why do you spend so much time washing the drinking glasses?" to which she replied, "To you, Stephen, they are just glasses. To me, they are the windows to the world." And so it was with her. She involved herself so completely in whatever it was that she was doing.

In the everyday way in which we live our life
We sign our signature to the things we do.
In so doing, we are calling out our name
~ both here and beyond.

My mother's wish for us would be that each of us would respond completely to our everyday circumstances with honesty and enthusiasm. What a world this would be! We would, in effect, be answering the call of spirit; illuming the world around us with our light and warmth. What a vibration of goodness and comfort we would collectively send forth. How much more quickly and safely would we pass this night through!

So many of us seem to be 'running near empty' in these times. We think (fret) that something outside of ourselves needs to 'come our way'. If we 'get this' or 'become that' things will get better is our common perception. This belief may be one great curse upon us! Instead of swirling in an eternal wish basket, we need to be celebrating the wonder of life in and around us. To paraphrase Kahil Gibron:

"Life has spoken and now we follow
Life gives nothing but itself, and takes nothing from itself
So, let us not be little of the much that we are.
May we not become the dawn unto our new day?"

Though you may have forgotten, and may place doubt upon these words, try to feel the message with your heart, and something familiar may quicken your pulse.

The Great Valley of Not Enough

In the beginning our being flew free
In the peace and grace of day
    However…
In this time of relative darkness
So many have entered the Great Valley
Of 'lost' and 'not enough'.
Thus the onward journey is threatened
As death seems to be entering

Our living rooms.
What was a home is now just a house—
The shutters are drawn tight against ourselves
And we are lost, as we shuttle about.

Let the kingdom be, in all the diversity we will see.
There will be me, there will be you
Then there is we, and the key is free.

Much of the above-noted darkness in the 'Great Valley of Not Enough' is harbored in the deep schisms and caverns of the mind. This faculty of our being is much too ascendant in many of our lives. If we really want to reach for the 'something more' of life and carry an inner confidence of its availability to us, we must relax our dependence on the purely mental and intellectual means of knowing and reclaim our most uniquely personal path to truth. How does it feel?

Yes, our mind has its place, but is it out of place? We cannot continue to trust in what we know by mind alone. Some things are best found (known) in the heart. This getting found imperative will have everything to do with returning feelings and enthusiasm to the life that remains with us.

Love this Life
    Or
Your navigation will be naught,
As naught will also be your wings.

Frankly, so much hangs in the balance in these times. It is inconceivable that we will not awaken from this sleep, connect with the splendor of life and respond to the call of our destiny. At this time only two alternatives affront us: succeeding or failing. Quitting is the only way we could fail, as we have already come this great distance and long in time.

Knowing where we now are
Upon life's journey
Has much to do with understanding
Where else we were.

So much of the power, so much of the awakening, seems to occur in communion—those intimate states of 'being-ness' that are often meditative or reflective times of openness. These times of communion find us essentially selfless, yet aligned with the eternal source of life and spirit. It is just at arms length if we are open to it. We are replenished by it. The sin of our time is to live in such a way as to withhold it from oneself.

Here again the misuse of the mind may be indicated. While we must rely on our mental sphere for directing and coordinating, we are so often (unaware, I am sure) employing our thoughts to separate and divide us from the very world to which we belong. Note the excessive use of judgments: someone is too old or too young, too white or too black, too fat or too thin, too liberal or too rigid, too tall or too short. When we allow our minds to entertain these judgments we are also diminishing the value of those around us, and thus withholding their warmth and light from ourselves. We thereby diminish our own value, as well.

> Look now into the heavens
> Stars of many colors and brilliance
> Sprinkle their radiance into the night sky.
> Those that are dim to us now
> May not be cast aside or plucked from the sky.
> The celestial perspective finds a place for them all
> Away from our question, "Why?"
> Those that seemed dim may now glow quite bright
> Those that were most brilliant may seem lost in the night
> Taken together their glow comforts our journey through the night
> Not one is wrong nor the other right
> Together they cast their warming, guiding light.

As we are able to lessen our dependence on the mind, with its incessant judgments and cause-and-effect truth testimony, a belonging to Something More may become evident to us. A warming sense of belonging to the all of life may begin to accompany us in our moment-to-moment living experience. In this warmth an intimate sense of connectedness (communion) with the world and the world of the unseen may begin to take root in our conscience. In this "rooting" we may become open to what life is asking of us in such an intimate way that we may seemingly feel her very breath upon us. Celebrate this. You have reconnected to the Source! This connection (communion) will allow us whatever we will allow ourselves. The habit of withholding may be broken. Darkness and unknowing may flee before this newly found purpose of life's light.

We will, indeed, be holding court with the significant! Our hopes and prayers will not be idle thoughts, but will rather be active connections to activities in our lives, and there shall be an answer! We will come to know our own individual design and purpose in this existence experience, allowing that we may become more intimate in life with a new-found joy and merriment in this living experience.

> We may now travel deeply
> Within our yesterdays and our tomorrows
> Throwing wide the windows of our being.
>
> What had been only a distant horizon
> Or a shadowy dream
> May become familiar again.
>
> We will have a renewed understanding of ourselves
> Both here and elsewhere
> As we live both here and elsewhere also.
>
> As we are able to wrap our arms around us
> We shall again breathe love and
> Deliver compassion absolutely.

We have begun again to move—the journey is renewed. A very clear parting from the Old into the New has begun. That which you were yesterday seems to have nearly vanished. This something new (more) now takes its place. With one manageable step in front of the next we are no longer stuck. An abiding conviction in our value and place in this existence experience will accompany us. This renewed and expanding reconnected self can only dare to imagine (remember) where we were.

> Existing apart from life
> Residing in the cold, distant, rigid existence
> Of never-ending night.

As we initiate this intimate connectedness, how might it feel? A subjective sense of wonderment may clue us to relax our focus on the outside world, take a deep breath, wait for a sense of warmth (never cold), which is often followed by perceptual images, condensed points of light and different, yet sweet and friendly sounds. For some these occur in the world around them; for others they seem to occur within their minds, or even a sort of psychic knowing. In all cases this psychic knowing is coming to you and from you simultaneously. It is as though we are entering a bridge from both ends. At this point in our connection with 'something more' our minds will invariably want to label (identify) this experience. Ultimately we will become better at suspending mind judgment and remaining receptive in an atmosphere of trust. Extremes of our 'mind talk' (labeling) may extend from a sense that we are touching our God all the way to a dismissal of the notion as hocus-pocus.

> Oh God, is that you calling?
> Yes, and remember that I am closer
> Than hands and feet.
> Seek now to know better yourself
> For I am in you
> And you are in me.

At times, as we attempt to part the curtains and open windows into other realities, our Earth self and senses can become overwhelmed.

There may be so much made available to us that we can't possibly respond to the all-ness of it. The overwhelming nature of this experience may cause us to step back—gingerly or hurriedly.

It was a mid-summer day in the early '70's. This particular year had been so full of the unusual. There was so much contact with the unseen—multiple crossovers into their worlds and back again. My relationship with Kathy, family, and graduate duties was suffering from the abundant other worldly communions. I was distracted! Still, I felt the imminent birth of something important. Perhaps a communion with Someone/Something Special—perhaps even Javunda. By day and night I remained vigilant in my wooded home. Almost to a fault I resisted being distracted from this Something I felt about me. Even my sleep was discouraged, as I felt a call and did not want to miss the "happening". I wanted to be available. Like an egg about to hatch, I felt it both within and about me.

Something did come crashing through. There, at the lawn's edge a great being did appear, with one powerful, glinting eye planted in the center of its head. The

face—almost human—was seemingly fitted within a metallic shield of sorts, perhaps as protection from the Earth's atmosphere and vibrations. His/her body also
appeared clothed in a bluish silver metallic-like covering, shimmering in its personal glow and presence.

This day's atmosphere was hot and humid with a light rainy mist falling like a
dog's spent breath upon one. But the visitor's shimmer glistened in the mid-after-
noon day, turning the mist and rain into vapors that rose about it. What an awe-
some presence! It was that for which I had waited, but it was too much. Before I
turned my head away it seemed to have something to say to me. But I could not
receive it—it was too much.

The most I knew about this startling being was a sound it delivered to
me—"Melix". It seemed like a great deal of energy and juxtaposed reality went
into the effort of this visit. If only I could have been stronger, extended my hand,
spoke or sang—anything. As quickly as I turned away, I felt ashamed. I turned
back again; it was gone. I've never quite forgiven myself for this missed opportunity. I had waited and longed for this visitation. I just was not prepared for the
immense power radiating from this alien. When we ask for, work for, and eventually manifest such a communion between worlds we must protect and drink
thirstily of the moment. I could not.

> Experience it, learn from it
> But do not
> Turn from it.

Yes, as in most communions, I knew something special had occurred. I knew
that this otherworldly contact was broken, the being was gone. My focus, like an
over-extended rubber band, returned to me and the planet Earth after some three
months or so of looking, preparing, waiting. I could give up, for now, the gelati-
nous connectedness to the beyond. I had really spent myself and tried the
patience of everyone around me as I prepared for this connection. Though it was,
indeed, a powerful visitation, I suffered a deep disappointment that I was not
more capable of interacting with this being—Melix. My personal recovery from
the shame and disappointment was facilitated by a return to my everyday responsibilities. However, even until now, there isn't a day that goes by that I don't
return to the inter-worldly traveler's image and wonder when we might meet
again.

What I took from this visit was a renewed sense of appreciation for my Lady,
my friends, and all things near to me. I returned my attention to the Earth with

new concern and renewed appreciation for the wonder of this world and the life so abundant, yet imperiled and stuck upon her. Was this what this splendid visitor left with me? Was this why it had come?

As with most suspended states of conscience (or communion), life will allow us to have them again, especially once we have done something with them. Opportunity will not withdraw, but in time will be even more available.

> As we continue along our way
> Each step will become that much surer
> Our courage that much greater
> And our personal course and intent
> That much clearer.

Just as we must walk before we can run, before we can ask for these unseen and otherworldly communions we must patiently develop an inner trust and connectedness with ourselves.

Perhaps nothing is more difficult in these times than to raise our awareness to the specialness of our being—The Sacred Self.

> In time you shall know
> How it is that we began
> How far it is that we have come
> And what it is
> We have left to be done.

I truly believe that if all the unique experiences and edge traumas of my life have any particular purpose, then I must leave this message with the Earth before my time here is done. This, more than anything, might be the message.

> The immense creative force
> Which has begun us and sustains us
> The interdependence between worlds and realities
> The splendor of living beings upon the Earth
> Albeit our fragility and, at times, limitations
> That all of life which entered into this journey

Remains still upon the vessel of Earth
And has a destiny for which we all thirst.

Did some traumatic event (as the tractor, in my case) need to occur in Melix's world of residence to bring him here? Is that what happened in the 33-acre field to the four-year-old farm boy? Was my edge experience set up? Was the tractor needed? Was that edge experience a necessary part of my introduction to Javunda, and thus my lifelong destiny in search of Something More along the earthen highway.

Melix's crossing over from some distant realm continues to amaze me. As he represented the outline of his world, I was the inline of our world. Two different realities had momentarily come so close in this communion between worlds. How did he accommodate to the design and laws of our planet Earth to essentially step through the veil? From where did he begin; what varieties and forms were parts of the transfer?

Excepting the single eye, and the shimmering metallic sort of skin, Melix's presence came as close to any to human form as I have personally experienced. Though I only observed this being from above the lilies and phlox at the lawn's edge, the part that I saw was clearly kin to us in one way or another.

My deeper sense tells me that at sometime in the distant past Melix's world and ours were connected. Did I not feel a sad longing in this being's powerful eye? Are not his people and their world waiting lovingly just beyond the great, dark sea? Won't it be something when we come together again?

Just two days after this alien's visit my Mother visited our cabin in Green Lane, PA. Still dazed, I recounted the visitation for her. Her read was this: How she would have given her right arm for such an experience! She felt that when I briefly turned my head from Melix that I broke the magnetic-like contact that was critical to his being here. For his very protection, leaving was critical to his preservation in this distant land. Perhaps for some days, and even weeks, our mutual attraction pulled and pulled upon Melix until he was able to breech the veil and enter into this world. Then, the duration of his stay became completely dependent upon the positive pull of my psychic and anticipatory magnetic force.

"But, Mom," I asked, "Did he not have a message for me?" "Stephen, I don't know," she replied, "But if another world or reality needs to speak with you they will find a way. As has happened already to you, they may pull you out of this land, beyond its orbit, and touch you on their terms."

This left me thinking of the tractor and other edge experiences: the initial pain involved in the going and the varied difficulties in returning. It made me wonder if it could be easier for me to bring them here. To this, my mother noted that this world was under some very specific designs and astral laws that are not very bend-able. Coming and going in and out of this world comes at a price. Whew! Didn't I know—Amen to that! She added, "For most people, Stephen, it would be death. But for you there has been some protection."

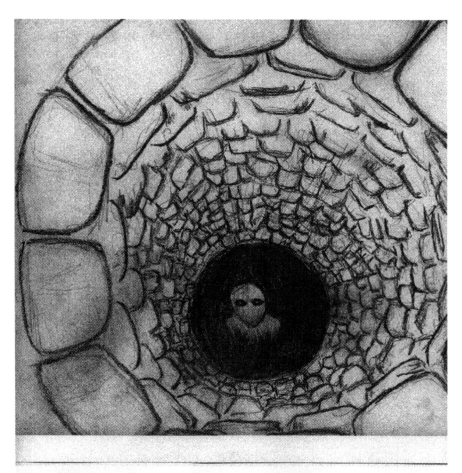

Getting Lost ... and Being Found

"Having fallen deep into the well, light could not shine from me or to me."

6

Getting Lost & Being Found

Without a feeling of specialness and trust in ourselves it is difficult to be connected to the Source. It is in this connectedness that the necessary energy and abundant knowing is made available to us. As an individual on life's incredible journey it is our challenge to seek out and discover this basic connection.

> The something more
> Asks
> That we allow a space
> While
> Coloring our place.

As we come to know ourselves as something special we may feel that we are also something more. Deep within the beat of our hearts and the intuitive center of our souls we come to better understand the rhyme and rhythm in the breath of life that surrounds us. Yes, in some ways these awakenings and discoveries are a solitary thing. The first step may be the most difficult.

> The beginning is the boldest
> Of steps
> But once we've taken this
> First step
> We are sure to take another
> And another...

As we reach, so are we received. Our song becomes more sweet; our colors become more clear. With each step, the light that shines will shine more clearly, and the beacon will beam more brightly. The shutters of the self are being opened; the curtain once closed is now being lifted. The light of understanding is entering the many rooms of our being. Some of the many facets and faces of the crystal self are becoming alive and are being illumed. The key of discovery may be at hand!

In the beginning of this awakening to the sacred self our best efforts may be opposed by habits of sleep and disbelief. Contemporary earth habits and values may be a suppressing or obscuring and weighty load upon us. On this matter, we must accept ourselves where we find ourselves, but we don't have to remain there (wherever that may be).

> Where are we now?
> This we know…
> We get there from here
> So on our journey
> We must go.

Here again I illustrate with someone (myself) who should not have become lost along his way, but did. So much of my (our) personal journey is about getting lost and (hopefully) being found.

Upon completing high school I headed off to college, essentially leaving the family farm. My mother recalled me declaring on my way out the door, "Well, Mom, I'll never work another hard day in my life." (Was I in for a shock! In fact, I created for myself some of the all-time hardest work I've ever had to do.)

Ten years after my out-the-door declaration while wrapping up my PhD at an urban university and in the third year of a wicked cocaine addiction I was as lost as a person could be. Yes, I was stuck! Light neither shined from me or to me. I had fallen into an empty well, and I was too spent to climb out. Once again, my mother, sister, and some others threw me a rope. There were significant others, however, who seemed content to push me even deeper into the well, throw dirt in upon me and leave me there!

The message that most of us need at times of severe "lostness" may be to "change the picture." This wisdom may have had its origins among the ancient Polynesians, who put it to frequent good use. No wonder they developed such early skills of navigation and sailing competence. If one island became inhospitable, they'd go find another one. I first became aware of this simple, yet compelling wisdom by way of a Kahuna, a teacher of Hawaiian truths, from Maui.

This was indeed the single most recurring directive to me from those who cared enough to help lift me from the well—to change the picture. This message, this challenge, which seems simple enough on the surface, can be daunting indeed to those most in need of its implementation.

What were they saying? Give up the $60.00 per hour job, the city lights, the cocaine, the pretty ladies? They must be crazy! Mom in particular went out of her way to support and nudge me back to myself. On one particular visit she framed her advise and concern with the following observation: "Stephen, you have the biggest feet in the family. God didn't put such big feet on you so that you could get lost in the halls of academia and waste those big feet up on a desk." (How well she knew me! My feet were, indeed, more likely to be found on a desk than under one.) And sure enough, a short time after this I was sitting in my Heller Hall office waiting for a favorite child client with my feet up on the cherry-wood desk, looking out the window, when I saw a sight that would forever change my life. My eye had caught the high-wire act of a tree man, dangling from his rope high in the canopy of a large campus tree. Wow! Light broke through the darkness! "Change the picture!" The trees! I loved the trees! I had worked with trees on occasion during my summer breaks from graduate school, and I always missed them when I had to return to the heavy academic and teaching load of the fall semester.

As a child, trees were my favorite natural objects. The woods were my favorite sanctuary next to the hayloft. Even my trusty, crusty friend Cheezer Wheezer lived in a large Hickory tree. During my times in the city I often found myself enjoying the large Sycamore trees down by the river. There, between the East River Drive and the Schuylkill River the many large, white-mottled trees afforded me a definite recuperative effect from the mentalism of the university, as well as the hurried demands of the large city. I would slowly walk among the scaling bark trees, loosening their shedding skins, and finding a restive peace of sorts before hurrying back the ten city blocks to a seminar or office appointment.

"OK, OK, trees, I hear you calling out my name!" But changing the picture would take a first step—a really big first step, as first steps usually are. I have noted so many people who have needed to change the picture but who just couldn't. Some have been short on will, courage, or vision; others have been literally blocked by others. For some of these people destiny sent, and they received, defining happenstance in their lives: injury, illness, economic loss or gain, etc., etc. In cases like these, they had no choice but to heed the call. The picture was changed for them. Often when people experience shocking or disastrous events in their lives, these experiences lead to positive and valuable changes. These changes can lead to contributions to ones self or others that could not have been imagined before the life-changing event.

The idea of changing the picture can work in big and little ways in our lives. For instance, I have used it effectively in helping others deal with nasty or demeaning dream states. Our conversation might be as simple as this: "Don't just lie there and allow the phantoms of darkness to steal your sleep and dump doubt on you. Get up for 15 minutes. Slip out of doors. Feel the dew-covered grass between your toes. Acknowledge the Earth, and send a brief 'Hello' to the heavens. Then return to bed and have your sleep once again." More to come about dreams...

Immediately following that day's treatment session with my young patient 'Billy' I felt compelled to get started with changing the picture. I knew that getting found—reconnecting with the breath of life—would be difficult. Two of my greatest hurtles would prove to be giving up my relationship with my young patients, and giving up the cocaine.

I went to the dean of the psychology department, Dr. Manning. "I am leaving the university," I stated with bare bones simplicity, "I have a cocaine addiction." In disbelief the dean argued against my decision. He offered me participation in a treatment program, a semester-long sabbatical, and several other compromise solutions. I protested, resisting vigorously, insisting that I must go. "You must hear me," I urged, as I pulled a small bottle from my pocket, "I've been using this white powder in practice and in teaching. I thank you for all that your department has done for me, but I know that I need to do this." He reminded me that I was already signed up for the next semester's classes. "We've opened up a large lecture hall, your teaching is so much in demand," he advised me, "We must find a way to get you through the year."

An inner power was already working. I was being freed up, being found. I was able to hold my ground!

This being found business is a 'now' door. When it opens we must be ready to step through (and in my case, run through). If the moment is missed, it may not be available again.

Enter, Gunther Bieler. Gunther was my special professor. He was the head of the developmental psychology department at the university, and he was exceptional in many ways. I worked in his research department. He oversaw my child psychology studies and was my dissertation supervisor. Early on I would deliver memos to his colleagues or fetch tuna (in water only) for his lunch. As the years of our association went by, Gunther and I became friends, and eventually I began seeing his son in therapy. I so admired Gunther. Perhaps one of the greatest affirmations I ever experienced was when Gunther traveled to my cabin in the woods to confide a very personal issue with me and to seek my guidance. Imagine! Gunther coming to me! Wow!

On the day of my big announcement in Dr. Manning's office, Gunther, having been summoned by Dr. Manning's assistant, arrived in time to see me still holding the little glass coke vile with the silver snorting spoon attached. My profusely sweating body was swaying to and fro. Even I could not believe what I was saying and doing. Gunther glanced at the bottle—he probably already knew about my chemical dependence—then he asked me to sit. I was so frozen in my determination I could not move; I could not sit; I could barely even speak.

Dr. Manning told Gunther of my problem and my determination to leave the university. Gunther shook his head and said, "Veeee must seeee about dis," his notable German accent even thicker than it usually was. Dr. Manning reiterated my obligation to the university, and my popularity as an instructor, noting the high evaluations I had been given by my students. "No one here, tenured or otherwise, has ever received such high evaluations," he pointed out in his best please-let-me-convince-you-to-stay voice. Reflecting on my students and my teaching assignments I knew it was something I'd miss. I also recognized, however, that much of the interest in me was an interest in the pieces of the "Something More" I inserted as I could in my lectures about love & hate, aggression, and death & dying. I had, in fact, been called down for not staying with the text material during the past semester. The complaint from one student regarding her interpretation of what I was saying went something like this:

> Too much light
> Can harm the sight
> Of one who has lived
> In the closet night.

All in all, however, I was impressed with how well my other-worldly visions and cloaked thoughts of other realities were received by the university students.

In an awkward moment, face to face with both Dr. Manning and Gunther, I realized I should have gone to Gunther's office first. But there can be a sense of urgency when we are escaping the deep well (being found) which does not lend itself to particularly well thought out planning. Mumbling an apology to Gunther, I told him I intended to come to his office immediately after speaking to the department chairman. Still I stood there, firm in my conviction that the trees were calling me, notwithstanding my discomfort at the breach of protocol.

Even then, an acorn of happiness was sprouting in my gut, where no life had been born to me in some time.

The pressure of the intensity of our meeting made this 'summit conference' seem to last an interminable period of time. Eventually, however, it did come to an end, with me agreeing to finish out the last two weeks of the fall semester. Gunther and Dr. Manning expressed their hope that after a little 'rest' I might one day return to the university. But I knew I had already 'stepped through'—I would not be back.

After all, the wisdom behind the message from Mom and others was not to change some of the picture, but to change the picture. Still, there was more to be done in completing this first step. I had lifted my foot from the dark side of life, and when I put it back down it had to be closer to the living room!

Other implications of this 'first step' would soon become obvious. There was the matter of economics. That winter was long and cold. We could not afford fuel oil, so we slept in front of an open fire. Our pipes burst and our walls cracked. It was sometimes hard to convince others that I was stepping into the light, while the foundation around me was crumbling and I was not always able to satisfy my most basic of needs. A local storekeeper seemed intuitively aware of my struggle, and one day offered us a bag full of 'scraps' to feed to our animals. If we didn't take them, he said, he would have to throw them away. When we got the bag home we found assorted meats, cheeses, sausages, and eggs all neatly wrapped in brown butcher's paper. It was the best food we'd had in a longtime. Thereafter, every week we picked up another bag of 'scraps', and each time the grocer thanked us for taking them off his hands. How special this man was. He gave us what we needed, and preserved our dignity at the same time. The store has long-since closed and the shopkeeper retired, but each time I pass that building I smile as I re-experience his gracious kindness.

Then there was the subject of the prestige I'd had in my position at the university. There was a lot of ego wrapped up in my academic activities, but eventually I would get over it. Ultimately it was just another shadow that had been keeping my inner light lean.

It was hard to part from my patients, Billy and the others. I brought them each to my cabin (what has become Happy Tree), and slowly we let go of one another.

One of the most painful frustrations for me at the university was my inability to cure almost anybody. Their pain became my pain. I seemed to have so little real success with them. We enjoyed one another's visits, but it bothered me that week to week their needs, dependencies, and general conditions very rarely improved. "Don't let it get to you. Don't take it home. Insulate yourself from it. The inner city is a tough place to work. We can't give these children families, and we can't change their neighborhoods." This was the advise I had gotten from my friend and colleague, Burt, when I expressed my frustration at failing to make enough of a difference in my young patients lives. Great advise, but I couldn't do it. I couldn't separate myself from them, my days from their days, my moments from their moments, my pain from their pain, my life from their lives. Their unresolved hurt stuck to me like glue, and its weight was more than I could bear.

Eventually the trees would offer much clearer evidence of my efforts and care. With trees the results were so much more apparent. If only one could remove deadwood from a child's mind as easily as he can prune it from a tree! If only peoples' hearts could "green up" as quickly as the canopy of a freshly fed tree.

The very last challenge in this difficult first step would be to free myself from the White Lady. The cocaine would take approximately six months of diminished usage. As I took my life to the trees the drug slipped away like a bad dream, never to return again. This is the power of changing the picture. I suspect that many people who are addicted to one thing or another could similarly benefit from such a change.

Clearly, getting lost is not something a person, culture, or world chooses to do. In effect, it is a consequence of one wrong step or sequence that leads to another, then another…In time, a direction that started off from a right beginning may go so far astray that a person may feel completely lost, his destination long-since forgotten. The worst of these scenarios occurs when the increments from light to darkness (right to wrong) are so small they are not even noticed. This kind of getting lost occurs over a great deal of time and often leads to a condition where the person who is lost comes to accept these conditions at face value, as "just the way things are."

Accepting the ever-diminishing
Qualities of light
Attempting to snuggle up
To the night
Everything is said
To be all right!

Letting go of the burdensome weight of being in the wrong place was a process indeed. Clearly, the infatuation with academia allowed so much to go wrong for me. The shadows crept slowly into my life, in such an incremental way that it was not obvious how goodness was being limited, or how the breath of life in me was slowly being extinguished.

The way of my life amounted to falling into a state of sin. Not the kind of sin that is the favorite subject of many religious sermons, but rather the one true sin, the great and debilitating sin of withholding—withholding life from oneself. This is the first sin, the one that allows all the other sins in! This is the condition that can most completely withhold the 'something more' from our lives. Know it now or not, without our forgotten faces and other places, the journey of our lives cannot be complete.

Withholding that of life from ourselves leads to an emptiness. Instead of living our lives from the inside out we ultimately try to compensate by living from the outside in. As this happens we are prone to needing the daily guidance of the Ten Commandments set down so long ago. Each one of these commandments cautions us against reaching out and taking from the world in a wrongful attempt to replenish something that seems to be missing from within us. In effect we are attempting to turn on a light that is surrounded by our own darkness.

Perhaps the biggest step on the climb out of the well is to forgive ourselves for having fallen in. Part of attaining this forgiveness is to undo some of the things, thoughts, and beliefs that were part of the wrongful attempt to live our lives from the outside in. As we do this the condition (sin) of withholding from ourselves is greatly diminished. Once again our life begins to flower and a fruit of our own is set anew. In so doing we again come to honoring ourselves and all life in the world about us.

> By shining so—
> Instead of being out of place
> We come back to be in place
>
> By shining so—
> So that a light might illume
> Any darkness out there
> Or whose warmth might soften
> Any hardness in here.

The overall value and exhilaration of being found (reconnected to life) is difficult to overstate. It is important to understand at least some of the conditions that allowed me to get so lost in the first place. Clearly the cocaine was the addictive agent most associated with depression, self-debasing behavior, wrongful thinking, and more. In the end it proved to be the most difficult shadow in the well for me to climb above. It was, however, not the only condition of my lostness. In a convoluted way, it even helped me recognize, and thus free myself, of the first and more menacing and entrapping addiction: academia (mentalness). For me it was a wrong highway that sequentially became more wrong the farther I traveled upon it. I had lost the critical balance between body, mind, psychic, and soul, and lived for quite some time exclusively in the thoughts and musings of the mind. For me, intellectualism was a lost and lonely highway that went nowhere well.

Most of my friends and family who would council me felt that the problem was in the powder. My mother would not be fooled. "Your feet need to be more firmly planted on the Earth!" She knew! She understood that the sequence of my getting lost occurred long before the use of cocaine. For her it had started with my exiting gloat when I left the family farm: "I shall never work another hard day in my life."

> The shadow is often cast
> At some distance
> From the object
> That obscures the light.

Day by day and week by week I diminished my use of cocaine, but in a single night I eliminated the outward trappings of ten years of academia. What a scene it must have been! It was a very cold and snowy day in early January. There was madness in the air. Still, it needed to be done. Clad only in my underwear I danced barefoot in the snow, tearing page after page from my textbooks, term papers, progress reports, and the first writing of my dissertation, serving them up one by one to the fire. The immensity of this occasion was not lost on me. I was so enflamed I never felt the cold. What a crazed man I looked to be! Oh, the things I needed to do to free up the knot in the shadowy ropes that had bound me. As the hours passed and my earthly load grew lighter page by page, I felt the weight of my confusion and despair being peeled away layer by layer. And there, underneath these many skins, I found something that had been a long time missing—myself.

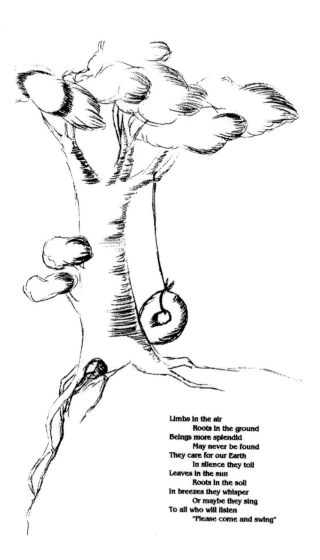

Limbs in the air
    Roots in the ground
Beings more splendid
    May never be found
They care for our Earth
    In silence they toil
Leaves in the sun
    Roots in the soil
In breezes they whisper
    Or maybe they sing
To all who will listen
    "Please come and swing"

7

The Wonder of a Tree & The _Secret of the Wood_

"The Wonder of a Tree"

Getting lost most frequently occurs when we live in such a way as to emphasize a small part of ourselves to the exclusion of our whole and many-faceted being. As we naively excel through one face of ourselves we may develop a shortsighted intolerance to the rest of our being, leaving us unbalanced and reaching out into the world to compensate for what we have already left behind. For me, it was to accentuate the mental and intellectual aspects of myself to the exclusion of the rest of me. This state could be likened to looking though only one window of one's personal mansion, leaving the rest to fog up and layer in dust. If we are not utilizing our other windows we are also not entering the many other rooms of our home, and we need them all to keep ourselves complete.

The 'something more' of this realm and other worlds is made available to us as we come back to our complete selves. At this point, today, nothing is as important to us as to see, and thus discover, within ourselves aspects of our life that may have been infrequently utilized or experienced, lost, or left behind. This process of discovery—understanding our complete or greater self—can be greatly facilitated by looking out from ourselves and into the natural wonder of the world. As we come to identify beauty and mystery beyond ourselves we are closer to finding it in ourselves as well. The most important conditions here are that we are willing to look, open to seeing, and willing to wonder.

Looking out gives birth to looking in.
Something else and something new
Will begin to be.

If we will see these things
> Then we will begin to see more.
Seeing these things, we begin to wonder
> Now, why won't we wonder more?
If we begin this wonder
> We can't help but open a new door.
Behind this door is more of our self,
> And we can't help but believe
> > There's even something more.

While there are innumerable avenues within creation's fabric that can lead us through the "back door", allowing us to discover ourselves; for me none could have done this better than have the trees.

During the process of discovering ourselves we also open ourselves to respond to what life is asking of us. What life is asking of us may at times seem extreme and unsettling. Clearly the journey has its obstructions. Sometimes it seems as if there is as much force against the completion of our purpose as there is force supporting it. At this time in western civilization the single greatest deterrent to our onward journey may be the emphasis our society places on the "bottom line." We measure the value of our efforts by economic gains and losses, power, control, etc. The value of the "top line"—purposeful living, environmental health, meaningful relationships, etc.—has been de-emphasized as the value of the bottom line is overstated.

In these times when the light of life is obscured and clouded over some means must be found to lift the darkness and part the fog. The call of life must go out and enter the minds and hearts of those among us. This call may at first seem painfully compelling and commanding. In responding to it we may find our everyday lives disrupted and changed. But later, if not sooner, value will be added to our lives and we will know that we are not being abandoned.

Such is as it was for me in the late summer of 1987 when I was responding to an environmental movement to save a community of native Oak trees. An old park in Southeastern PA had heretofore been the protector of 54 massive 300+ year old White Oak trees. In recent years the park had closed its gates to the summer picnic crowds, and the magnificent tree beings had become vulnerable to the economic powers that be. As part of a larger area-wide water reallocation project, these trees were condemned and scheduled to come down to make room for a water treatment plant. When I head of the authorities' intention to remove these trees my heart ached. Just the previous Halloween I had spent the night among them celebrating their long and glorious lives under a frosty fall moon.

I was contacted by a water project protestor, who informed me that I needed to join a massive protest or the trees of Wilderness Park were going to be lost. I could not really identify with the tactics and nasty nature of these water project protestors; yet I could also not stand by and do nothing to try to save these trees. I joined one of their protests, and soon I was being hauled away with about 50 other protestors to spend some time in the County Prison System. Being charged and held over for trial on a trespassing charge further fanned the fire that had ignited within me. In a mysterious sort of way I became a voice for the trees, and they, in turn, empowered me to hold my ground. At the time of our hearing, Judge Traub extended the option of "purging" to gain our release. Purging would essentially involve admitting wrong-doing and swearing before the court that we would no longer engage in such activities. To my amazement, most of my fellow detainees elected to purge and go free, but a couple other serious individuals and I held our ground and remained in jail. Over the next few days the others, too, gave in to the easy way out, and I remained in jail alone. I could not believe that those who had protested so loudly could sell their convictions so cheaply when it came to experiencing some personal inconvenience!

This fire of conscience burned within me as I stated in court that I could not allow these trees to fall before me. A statement of purpose poured from my eyes as I tearfully told those in attendance that technology had outdistanced conscience, and that we needed to stand in the way of the bottom line thinking of these times, because the future of our Earth was hanging in the balance. Overwhelmed by emotion and intent, the "Voice for the Trees" was remanded to the County Jail, where I was sentenced to remain unless and until such time as I chose to purge.

Finding the state of life and the treatment in jail to be intolerable, I soon began to refuse food, except for a teaspoon of maple syrup per day mixed in a cup of water. Forty five days later, and about 65 pounds lighter, Judge Traub ordered my release. "We can't afford to have anybody die in here," was his practical explanation for his abrupt change of heart. Nevertheless, I continued my fast, because the future protection of the trees of Wilderness Park had not been assured.

About 10 days later I was awakened from a restless sleep by Kathy. She informed me that there were limousines in the driveway and she thought I should get up. The Authorities had arrived with some chicken broth and a white flag in hand. "Eat of this broth and the trees shall be spared," was their cryptic but timely message. Instead of wiping out this special piece of Eden the authorities would condemn a 50-acre abandoned cornfield for their treatment plant. The answer had been there all along.

So, life had balanced the scale of helpful relief. The trees had lifted me from a very deep, dark personal well, and now I had the opportunity to speak for and protect some of them. During this long and difficult fast my body was forever weakened and my vision permanently scarred. But never did I hunger for anything but a meaningful resolution to my mysterious call to stand up and be a voice for the trees.

There is so much wonder in a tree. The magic of its grand design is never more available than when one sits by a wood fire. Presently, in the mid-winter of '04 during an extended cold snap I have answered a call to write some of this stuff down. "Stephen, write it down, because if your don't write it down, when you're gone it's gone." To this beckoning I have responded, and I have benefited greatly in my journey from the dancing flames of a warming fire in my open-door stove. I am certain that the "melting" of the wood is an abiding companion in this endeavor.

"The Secret of the Wood"

In so many ways a fire can unlock the different layers of a tree. That trees are what they appear to be is obvious enough, but they are also much more. It is my belief that they often offer themselves as repositories of spirit life, life that is released in the form of tap screws. As wood tissue is burned away, one may distinguish these releases as certain types of embers that flash and glow in their own unique ways. Some of these spirit embers may represent the essence of many different life forms that, at one time, existed upon the Earth. As a member of life's existence experience passes on (dies), where does its essence go? Does it depart to some distant realm? To Heaven? Or Hell? I think not. I am convinced that all who once dwelled upon this planet still reside here in one form or another. Many, I believe, have found residence (a resting place) in the trees. Here they quietly sustain themselves, maybe even assisting the arboreal structure in some way. These resident spirits should not be confused with the energy forces that actually grow the tree. Other reservoirs of the energy of spent history include fossil fuels, minerals, vapors and gasses. If these 'resting' spirits are altered, such as put under pressure or set afire, all will express some form of heat or light—qualities central to life itself.

If we accept that there was intention and purpose to our inception, then we must also acknowledge that there is purpose to our journey, and to our personal and collective lives over time and space.

> Life into darkness sent
> God's grace in creation lent.

Much of what this journey (mission) is about has taken us to a place far from home (our inception). There is no jumping ship! The realization of our journey is also our destiny:

> That one day with a beginning
> But not an end.

As we undertake our excursion over the course of time and space, our Earth has no way to ferry us either back through the darkness or ahead toward the unknown. Like it or not, we are all kin here upon this one vessel. From the time of our birth and throughout the expression of our life we give a face and a name to our energy form. At the same time we are serving the ship (the Earth) and shaping the voyage. The sails on our ship are filled by the collective breaths of life from her voyagers as we move from port to port on our life's path. One by many we come into this existence experience. We take our places and serve upon the deck of life. Then, as our time and duty are completed, we withdraw into the inner hold of our ship, Earth. During this time we continue on in a myriad of ways. Spirit and essence are recorded, stored, and preserved, creating a template of sorts that, in time, may again be awakened for another journey in a new shape and a later time.

At this juncture I return to the subject of the wood and the fire. It is in the wood, I believe, that many of these spirits are harbored and protected. When the wood of a tree is introduced to a fire, the transition from solid to fluid is begun, and many secrets and mysteries may unfold. Along with the release of the sun (light and warmth), there is also smoke. The smoke may represent the negative qualities that the tree assimilated during its life, such as toxic gasses or errant chemicals. No living being has ever existed on this Earth that has not been exposed to and thus consuming of some of the negative that is so prevalent in this realm we travel through. Darkness, pain, suffering, sadness—each is an unavoidable part of living. It simply comes with the territory. In the case of the tree, the wood is cleansed of these impurities as it burns. The heat from the fire is able to lift this smoke and disburse it over and above the vessel. At the same time the spirit of the tree and spirits resting in the wood are fired and freed to express themselves, then seek new quarters. In a distinct departure from the fire itself these spirit beings (tap screws) have a dynamic quality of movement and presence that often amazes me. In one recent experience I laid some sticks of wood across a bed of coals that were left from the previous night's fire. I could not see the embers or coals, since the fire had settled into a gray cover of ashes, but the heat in the stove and the warmth above the ashes revealed their presence. Soon a curl of smoke rose between the freshly placed sticks, and in a short while a magical sort of flame lifted and moved about. I soon realized I was watching a fire fairy begin her dance upon these slivers of Walnut wood. How beautiful she was as she moved from end to end of the wood! She appeared simply as a double-tongue of 2"-3" flame, but the dynamic nature of her presence was clear. Upon the wood she moved and swayed. Her color was a deep orange. Smoke surrounded this double-wicked flame, but it could not suppress or extinguish her. I was spellbound. Clearly a being had just been freed from the wood, and she was expressing herself with exquisite beauty. It was just her and the smoke for 5 or 7 minutes. Then, all of a sudden, the entire contents of the stove burst into flame. Every piece of wood was equally burning. Instantly the fire fairy rose above the fire, burst into 20 or 30 sparklers, left the stove, encircled my head, reverberated in my shack, cackled a word and vanished. Clearly life lives and expresses on every level of our world. Incredible!

If we will just practice the looking, spirits will happily express themselves. It matters not whether we look lazily into the sky or transfix our gaze upon a fire, we will see them there.

> Above in the vapors and the clouds
> > Below in the coals and embers of the fire
> > > We will see them there!
> As we shall acknowledge them
> > We shall also be received by them.
> And each and every one will see
> > What once was earlier conceived.

We must be careful not to focus too strongly. We need to allow our eyes and our senses to relax, so that something special might come forth to express itself.

> The journey continues on
> > The dark sea
> Until such time
> > As we will see.

If one chooses to understand the wonder of a tree, I believe one must observe its finished heartwood, or be present during its burning process. The heat that is released from the wood is, in essence, the sun being returned to the world. Part of the mystery of a tree that gives it a special status to me is the way it builds itself upon the energy from the distant sun.

> The golden orb
> > Is a tree maker.
> Those who are warmed
> > By the wood
> Are golden flame takers.

It is so true. The mystery and magic of a tree are so real. Throughout the life of a tree she provides for the world in which she lives, all the while taking nothing from it. She serves the vessel well.

> She is an Oxygen maker, a habitat provider.
> She clothes the land and buffers the Earth's skin
>> From harsh sun and strong winds.
> She cools us when our world is hot,
>> And cloaks us in her warmth when winter is cold.

With all of this said, the wonder continues. If we pull a large tree from the Earth and blow every particle of soil from every microscopic root; even though we may measure seven tons of material (wood), the soil around it has not been diminished by even an ounce from the time the tree's seed first took root. In fact, there is a little <u>more</u> earth than was there at the beginning.

How can this be so? She is a unique and giving being, indeed. She is a miracle maker. Through photosynthesis, a yet to be completely understood process, she builds herself from the sun. Whew! True, she borrows elements and water from the Earth, but all of these, plus a little more, are returned in her leaf drop, fruit giving, and transpiration. She cools our world when we are hot, and warms us in winters cold. As I burn her in my stove she gives back the sun that nourished her, and her warmth comforts me.

If we humans were more like trees, this Earth (our vessel) would have a much more certain future. A tree so manages its life that it would behoove us to try to be more like it. Think about it. The very qualities that so preoccupy us today are already natural to a tree. We crave longevity; the trees are the longest-lived of all. No other life form so endures. A single Bristle-cone Pine tree in California's Sierra Nevada Mountains was 'born' approximately 3,000 years before Christ, and still lives today, witness to 5,400 years of continual existence. We value independence; trees found in a forest maintain their own world constantly, without need for external intervention. Yet they are continually giving to the world to which they belong. We treasure size; no other species is grander than the tree. Taken as a whole, trees may represent the most successful of life forms. And they are a key element necessary to the health and well being of the planet.

> Still, it saddens me to see how vulnerable
>> These grand beings are
> To being felled by man's technology.

In nature's ferocity they're fired.
Still, as they die they give us this
    "Make a dwelling for yourself
    Shingle your roof, then build a shelf.
    Take my wood into your hearth
    When you are warmed,
    Discover yourself!

We think of trees as hard. They are not. Their wood is hard to the touch, but the living part of the tree—the cambium—is as fragile as our skin. In a matter of speaking, a tree is only ever one year old. That which we see, the visible tree, is really its 'firmed up' history—the tree of yesterday and past years. In a thin soft layer just under her bark lives her life-giving, growing cambium. Here is where she divides and multiplies and adds to herself season by season and year by year. She builds up over and around herself, creating a wonderful, strong and sturdy being. But the truly dynamic aspect of a tree is quite fluid. That is the spirit is in her, of her, and all about her.

    Life need not always
        Be firmed up.
    Much of it is fluid.

She is built from the fluid waters of the Earth and the borrowed, somehow captured, electrons of the sun. Her life is essentially a result of the exchange of gasses. The building of carbons takes place, to be sure, but these are ultimately given back in the fluid forms of heat and light.

In my comings and goings among the trees I have come to believe that they are unique beings capable of simultaneously belonging to different worlds. Clearly I have seen otherworldly life forms come and go through them, as they did back on the farm on the day that Judy surprised Cheezer-Wheezer, and he so easily was able to slip into the base of the Hickory tree. There was no visible door there, but Cheezer-Wheezer was readily received.

I most fondly remember a time shortly after my maniacal dance around the fire that consumed my texts and thesis when my lady, Kathy, and I were standing outside our country cabin, having just returned from a nighttime walk. It was a magical mid-summer night, with ample sounds of evening and a liberal sprinkling of tap-screws. I felt or heard a presence at the woods edge. I shined my flashlight, and from the sturdy base of a Shagbark Hickory tree a heavily cloaked lady and her daughter emerged. There was a great deal of chatter between them, and some scolding from the Mom. As the volume and intensity of the exchange grew, the Mom deftly swung what appeared to be an old fashioned loaf of hearth-baked bread, landing it with a dull thud on the girl's thickly skirted behind. Then, as easily and obviously as they had exited one tree they entered another a few dozen feet away. Were they hobbits or gnomes? Certainly they were little people-like beings.

"Did you see what I saw?" we simultaneously asked as we entered our cabin. We compared the details of our individual experiences and found them to be strikingly alike. There was so much to be taken from this experience. How clear it was to both of us. How non-threatening and comfortable it was to perceive. It was, we have discovered, unusual in that two different people observed exactly the same rendezvous with the unusual at exactly the same time.

> Another reality opened up to us
>> And we looked similarly in.
> Little people from another world
>> And another time
>> Is what we saw.
> It wasn't simply a dream.

When we enjoy sitting by a fire, we are part of a very interesting transforma-tion. What was once a solid (wood) is altered by a flame and departs as heat and vapor, leaving its minerals and carbon dust behind. I have always been intrigued by the spirit-like elemental life that escapes during this process. This mysterious essence appears to the eye as a concentrated glow and to the ear as a chiming hiss, both coming from seemingly solidified embers. To me, this is the ultimate release of the concentrated energy that initiated birth and managed the life and design of this tree (or being).

My fascination with this transfer of energy has led me to spend countless trea-sured moments observing it. I have found that the experience of this energy release varies greatly from wood piece to wood piece and from tree to tree. The numbers of releases, colors and parting actions may be quite different. Although I am not entirely clear as to the composition of these escaping energies, I am cer-tain that in the melting of wood there is more than heat, light, and smoke released. On more than one occasion I have witnessed these elementals (tap screws, embers) leave a fire in darting fashion, only to circle and return to the flame. In one particular incident while burning Mulberry wood one such ember exited my stove, darted about my office shack, returned slowly past my ear emitting an interesting word-like sound, and with a popping, whizzing dance reentered the open door of my woodstove.

So trees, like all of life, owe their presence to a sustaining source from which all of us draw our life energies.

> Creation and the Bread Maker
> Shaker
> Baker
> Taker.

It is my belief that it is these discharged aspects, these elemental spirit embers, which return the very essence of creation to itself. The rest of what makes a tree a tree is utilized from the sun (light) and the vessel (Earth), and what a wonderful design and function a tree has!

> Spirit sets the power
> Of creation free.
> Her elementals build and tie
> It to a tree.
> Even within the rigid confines of a tree
> This life continues to be.
> Quietly and effectively this tree
> Serves this vessel upon the great sea.
> And when its time has come
> And its life is done
> She returns all
> Even the sun.
> The essence living in her wood
> Earth's angels might become
> Now a fire that's warming me
> Sets the angels free.

8

The Sting

My most recent excursion into the beyond occurred two years ago as a result of a massive attack of yellow jackets. My most intimate and complete contacts with the unseen realms of existence have always resulted from my 'edge' experiences. Others might call these 'close calls' or 'near death' experiences. For whatever reason I have had a series of these 'edge' experiences throughout my life. On each such occasion the going from Earth and the coming back have been very painful and overwhelming. These 'edge' experiences for me imply a complete transition of mind, soul, and psychic between worlds, and from these experiences I am left with a complete conviction of the "something more" of life.

For me, the pain I felt occurred most acutely during the moments of taking leave: the moment the tractor passed over me, the instant I was hit broadside by an out-of-control automobile, the split-second it took to be hit by lightning, the torturous minute instants of being stung by hundreds of angry bees. The feeling of being overwhelmed, and sometimes that of being depressed, occurred during and after my 'reentry': waking up in a hospital bed, emerging from a coma, beginning the long climb from devastation to revitalization. It was once said that to enter the heavens we must be able to pass through the eye of a needle. When one of these edge experiences sets upon us it feels not unlike making this unlikely passage—both there and back again.

The day of the yellow jacket attack I felt pain the likes of which I had never before known. I had been grading an unruly section of my nursery using a skid steer equipped with a bucket. I was scooping up sections of lumpy dirt from high spots, moving them to spots where there were depressions, and then back dragging the bucket to smooth it all out. Although Kathy had been unusually insistent that we spend a family day together having a late season swim and a picnic, I insisted on moving forward with my project, telling her it would only take a short time. Indeed the climate was perfect that day, as were the soil conditions, and my little nursery project was well on its way to being completed. Suddenly the bucket of my tractor came into contact with a large and aggressive nest of very angry yellow jackets, hundreds of which emerged and swarmed around me—their archenemy—in the cage-enclosed cab of my vehicle. Besides the obvious problem of me having destroyed their home, this event happened in the late summer when these ground wasps seek out an animal target to attack and kill from whose decaying body they feed their developing larvae. So, the bees were naturally more aggressive, there were many of them, and I was a captive adversary at a time when they were looking for a victim. I would pay the price for messing with them, and I would feed their children, too.

At first it felt like hard stones or ice hitting my face and body; then the fire of their many stings became obvious. They came in such numbers that I could not see beyond them even as I climbed out of my protective cage and jumped to the ground. The desperate nature of my position was immediately apparent as this venomous, aggressive community of beings covered my body like a furry, humming carpet. I knew I might not survive this onslaught, but with my children standing close by I knew I had to try. My instinct was to head for the banks of the Ridge Valley Stream that runs through my nursery and that lay about 100 feet from where the attack began. I ran, but as the massive doses of venom reached my heart (and maybe also my mind), I called out to God to take me. I lost consciousness just feet from my destination and pitched forward into the stone driveway. Somehow, though, from my face down state of recumbence I was lifted and thrust into the stream. I regained consciousness bobbing in the stream, using my hands to rip the carpet of bees away from my skin. At one point I noticed their many bodies floating downstream with the currents, and navigating the same path was the hat I had worn only moments before. As I saw the hat I simultaneously felt the burning in my scalp, as the survivors of the dive into the water stung the only part of my body that was still exposed—the top of my head. I submerged my head for protection, and emerged only briefly to catch my breath. The struggle continued for a number of minutes. I couldn't believe how these critters could still deliver their punishing stings even under water. An entomologist who later came to view the site told me that yellow jackets can deal with being in water for a number of minutes, and that, in fact, water is essential for them to properly digest their kill in order to feed their larvae. It turns out that the most effective thing to do in the midst of an attack is to seek out a shady thicket to run through as a means of escape. It's hard to know whether or not that knowledge would have altered the events of that day. My reaction was instinctual, my intellect primitive, my destiny in the hands of some power not my own.

I had been working with three of my children that day—Orrian, Meurie, and Jaeilyn, and at some point I became keenly aware of them standing on the bridge about 35' from where I had ended up in the water. My daughter called to me that I had to take some medicine. It seemed incredible to me that my child would have this medicine in her hand, but I was in a haze and didn't pursue the unlikeliness of this in my mind. It turned out that my wife, returning from the grocery store, had driven down the road toward us to inquire as to our readiness to begin our picnic. Jaeilyn had run to meet her and breathlessly told her of my plight. She immediately drove to the house and got large doses of Benedryl and Ibuprophen, which she sent back in Jaeilyn's frantic grasp on the 4-wheeler with instructions to make me take it all immediately. I drank the pills down with stream water, and as the remaining stragglers from the swarm subsided, my lovely children helped me from the water. I marveled that they had not been harmed. They were there the whole time but not one was stung. Kathy had stayed at the house to prepare me a baking soda bath and assemble the antidotes and medicines I would need to deal with stings. She knew me too well to think I would agree to go to the hospital. She drove back down to get me, but for reasons I still don't understand I insisted on being driven up on the 4-wheeler by one of the children. Perhaps I wanted them to know just how large a part they had played in my rescue, and allowing them to deliver me to my residence was my way of letting them follow through on their efforts.

Throughout this experience I was elsewhere—the beyond—while I was also here. In a very unusual way I would flip-flop between worlds over a period of 8 to 10 Earth days in a way that I never had before. I was clearly in and on the world of Javunda, even as I was aware of being here. I was living completely in two different worlds simultaneously. Whew! I had never experienced this in such a living, coordinated way before. I found that it was necessary to listen to and look out for clues so that I might know which reality I was responding to.

Clearly, the land of Earth and the space of Javunda are different in design and operate with different laws. Even now, as I sit before my woodstove recalling these events, the depth of experience we are able to reach and the limitless nature of our conscience impress me. We can reach out and touch different realities, and we can see into distant worlds.

Although my answer was a foregone conclusion, Kathy asked me several times if I thought I should go to the hospital. I was still somewhat ambulatory, and her car was still running in the driveway. The local hospital is only about 7 minutes away, and with the children's help she knew she could get me in the car and drive me there. She also knew that as I became more toxic from the stings it might not be so easy to move me around. Despite the practical nature of her request, I refused. I was sure I was ending my journey on this Earth, and I only wanted my children and my wife around me when I breathed my last breath.

I don't remember getting into the house and Kathy and the kids removing my clothes and shoes and leading me upstairs to the waiting bath. They told me my clothes, especially the cuffs of my socks were filled with bees, many were dead, and some were dazed but still alive. I do remember sliding down into our over-sized bathtub and feeling the warm, soothing water caress my flaming skin. I soaked there for a long time, the baking soda soothing my wounds and drawing the many stingers to the surface where they could be wiped away. Meanwhile, the Benedryl took effect and that, in combination with the adrenalin from the attack and the toxins from the stings made me somewhat sedate and slowed time so that each moment seemed exaggerated, each thought seemed monumental. I glanced at the water and saw the many tiny stingers floating on its surface. These hundreds of miniscule black needles sharing the bath water with me enumerated the enormity of the attack.

When it came time to exit the tub and make my way to my bed I found that I could not move. I had excruciating pain in my back and it took the strength of all of my children and my wife to get me out of the tub and travel the few feet to my bed. The burning from the bees had subsided somewhat, but the pain in my back was unbearable. I found out later that I had torn a muscle in my back, probably as I was hastily exiting my skid steer out in the nursery field.

This first night of the attack was extremely difficult for my wife and children. I drifted in and out of consciousness, back and forth between another world and here. When I was here I was screaming out in pain and anguish; when I was there my family thought they were losing me. Their vigil by my bedside lasted through the night and into the wee hours of the morning. At some point in my stupor I called each of my children to me and told them I would allow them one last request—something I could arrange to get for them that would be a cherished gift from Papa. Shetlinn requested a dirt bike—the grown up kind that could be ridden on the road when he was old enough to drive. Orrian reminded me that he needed his own space, a bedroom to call his own. Orrian had adopted a tiny little space in the attic eves of our house above our front porch as his room, rather than share a space with one of his siblings. He was a teenager now, though, and he had outgrown this little cubbyhole. Meurcie reminded me that, of course, she wanted a horse. When it was little Jaeilyn's turn he hopped up onto my belly and pried my eyelid open with his fingers to be sure that I was awake when he made his request. He said, "Papa, I want to have a puppy with saggy lips," and as he said it he took his fingers and wiggled them down beside his own lips. The image of this child with his beautiful, child-like request will remain with me forever.

As I talked with my children I felt pulled to stay in this realm; although throughout the night I found myself having clear and powerful contacts with another world, and the impressions were vibrant and beckoning. At some point I acquiesced and agreed with my family to seek medical help if I lived through the night, for that would be a sign that I was meant to endure here a bit longer. Still, the world of Javunda—the Something More—remained an intriguing entity, and I remember traveling readily between the two realities, sometimes even existing in both simultaneously. The wee hours of the night gave way to the pre-dawn hours of the morning, and it was the agreed upon time to call the ambulance.

My next recollection was opening my eyes to see a monstrous yellow jacket approaching me with its huge stinger approaching my arm. As the swirling fog in my brain cleared a bit I came to understand that it was a doctor approaching me with what became one of many needles. I was hooked up to IV's, given pain medication and muscle relaxants, antibiotics, and anti-inflamatories. My extremities were packed in ice; my vital signs were taken by machine. Thus began my 10-day hospital stay.

During this time of drug and venom induced stupor the spirits and vibrations of some very wonderful and giving people looked into my psychic. They soothed and comforted me, cared for my heart and kept me alive. Later I would be told of some very interesting conversations I had with my guests. Though they were visiting me here, on Earth, I was often visiting with them from somewhere else, the world of Javunda.

Time passed, my physical devastation healed, and once again I was retuned completely to my existence on planet Earth. I was amazed how heavy my earth-body felt, and I missed the weightless, timeless world of Javunda. Still, I was glad to be back. I could not yet walk, but my family and friends aided me in navigating my home and the place of Happy Tree. One of my favorite memories of that time is being transported around the grounds of Happy Tree lying on my back in a wooden cart being pulled by a four wheeler driven by one of my children. I so enjoyed watching the tree tops go by, and the cloud formations taking shape in the endless sky. On more than one occasion I would see the vaporized likenesses of dear ones looking in from the place of Javunda. Though I seemed far away I also felt close as we signaled one another, "So long for now," from beyond the veil. It took me quite some time to get past the enormity of my experience, both here and in the beyond. It was a pivotal point in my life, and to this day I am still coming to terms with its many lessons.

As I ponder the impressions I am left with I am convinced more than ever that the Earth and her inhabitants are inextricably connected with a world or worlds beyond, and that the mutual benefits of such a connection are many and profound. How is it, then, that so few people here on Earth can see it? How do they go through their lives thinking that this is all there is? And, if they do, how do they find happiness in the passage of time or hope in the future ahead? Why do I constantly see a yearning for "something more" in the eyes of strangers? Have they forgotten that it is all one? Don't they know that the breath of existence belongs to us all, always?

> Have we all forgotten?
> The journey is so long, the nighttime so difficult,
> We best do what we do
> When we do it all together.

9

Trouble at Sea

✦

(a parable)

In the middle of a long night the sailors struggled against a great storm. With their sails already tattered, a loud crack sounded and the main mast fractured. With deep darkness all around them the vessel listed, and seawater swept over them.

The people retreated into the hold of their vessel. In intermittent moods of fear and despair they alternated calling out to God and cursing at the devil. Some of the sailors tore at the already weakened timbers of the boat in order to start a small fire to warm themselves. Ghostly faces gathered around the flames. Some pleaded that God not forsake them.

Suddenly the sea was stilled. The ship righted itself and the winds abated. They had met the eye of the storm. A handful of men made their way back to the deck. As they gazed into the darkened sky a lone star shining brightly greeted them. A voice spoke to them. Perhaps it was from within them, it seemed so near. Was there a hidden spirit upon this ship? Was God somehow along on this great voyage?

"Sailors, why do you call out to me? Have you forgotten? Now, when things are most urgent you must reach down within yourselves! Yes, your courage will satisfy the demands upon you and your vessel if you will only have faith in your destiny."

"Do not look up to the heavens for me. I am not there. Likewise, do not seek me at the bottom of the sea. Are you lost from me? Please remember, as it has been since the beginning, I am in you, as you are in me."

"The well-being of you ship is integral to the safe completion of this journey. You must not burn her timbers to warm yourselves. A fierce conviction of the importance of this journey shall be fired by your faith, and from your mission you will gain warmth aplenty."

"Yes, but we are thirsty," came their anguished cry. "Already some of us have fallen ill from drinking the salty water from the sea."

"There is fresh water enough stored in casks just below your deck. Drink only of this water; do not take from the sea."

"Brother, Sister, Mother, Father, Guardians, Keepers, Seekers, and some Deceased Speakers, trust that what is begun will be done! Carry on now, Sailors. Know that you will outlast this tempest. All hands on deck to care for your ship! Soon this long, but not endless, journey will be completed, and you will have passed the night through. Your vessel, anchored in protected harbors, will release you unto a great and giving land. It will be such a place where life lives and death is not even known. It will deliver you into a land where love and compassion bloom all around; where joy is a song sung so completely it seems to always be in the air.

And along with all this love,
This world will send to you
a life without an end.

The Beginning

978-0-595-34665-3
0-595-34665-0

CPSIA information can be obtained at www.ICGtesting.com
Printed in the USA
BVOW011131150312

285180BV00001B/77/A